# The Final Kingdom

# The Final Kingdom

The kingdom that will put an end to all others,
and it itself shall stand forever.

by Joshua Stone

First Edition: 2021
Copyright © 2021 Joshua Stone
Contact: TheFinalKingdom@Yahoo.com
Social Media: BibleUnited@YouTube.com

ISBN: 978-1-7370700-2-3

All rights reserved. No part of this publication may be reproduced, stored in a retrieval system, or transmitted, in any form or by any means, electronic, mechanical, photocopying, recording or otherwise, without the prior permission of the author.

All Scripture quotations, unless otherwise indicated, are taken from the Holy Bible, New International Version®, NIV®. Copyright ©1973, 1978, 1984, 2011 by Biblica, Inc.™ Used by permission of Zondervan. All rights reserved worldwide. www.zondervan.com The "NIV" and "New International Version" are trademarks registered in the United States Patent and Trademark Office by Biblica, Inc.™ Scriptures marked NCV are taken from the New Century

Version®. Copyright © 2005 by Thomas Nelson, Inc. Used by permission. All rights reserved.

Scripture quotations marked ESV are taken from The Holy Bible, English Standard Version® (ESV®), copyright ©

2001 by Crossway, a publishing ministry of Good News Publishers. Used by permission. All rights reserved.
Scripture quotations marked CEB are quoted from the Common English Bible, copyright © 2010 by the Common English Bible http://www.commonenglishbible.com/. Used by permission. All rights reserved.

Scripture quotations marked NLT are taken from the Holy Bible, New Living Translation, copyright ©1996, 2004, 2015 by Tyndale House Foundation. Used by permission of Tyndale House Publishers, Inc., Carol Stream, Illinois 60188. All rights reserved.

Scripture quotations marked NASB are taken from the New American Standard Bible®, Copyright © 1960, 1962, 1963, 1968, 1971, 1972, 1973, 1975, 1977, 1995 by The Lockman Foundation Used by permission. www.Lockman.org.

Scripture quotations marked CEV are from the Contemporary English Version Copyright © 1991, 1992, 1995 by American Bible Society, Used by Permission.

# Dedication

This publication is dedicated to God Almighty; for unto Him, all things exist.

# Contents

Preface .................................................................. iii

Introduction ............................................................ v

Part One – Salvation

    Chapter 1:1 – Struggles, Trials, and Strife ................... 1

    Chapter 1:2 – What Is Sin? ........................................ 9

    Chapter 1:3 – Trees of the Garden ........................... 19

    Chapter 1:4 – Why We Suffer .................................. 27

    Chapter 1:5 – The Image of God ............................. 35

    Chapter 1:6 – What Is Salvation? ............................ 41

    Chapter 1:7 – The New Creation ............................ 53

Part Two – Eschatology

    Chapter 2:1 – Chronology ....................................... 63

    Chapter 2:2 – Holy Days ......................................... 75

    Chapter 2:3 – Time of the End ................................ 83

    Chapter 2:4 – Seventy Weeks ................................. 93

    Chapter 2:5 – The Day or Hour ............................. 101

    Chapter 2:6 – The Temple Sanctuary ..................... 109

    Chapter 2:7 – Resurrection .................................... 117

## Part Three – A Witness

Chapter 3:1 – The Israel of God ............................. 127
Chapter 3:2 – The Great Apostasy ........................ 135
Chapter 3:3 – Two Witnesses ................................ 147
Chapter 3:4 – 7 Eyes, 7 Spirits, 7 Lamps ................ 161
Chapter 3:5 – The Cup of Christ ............................ 171
Chapter 3:6 – The Correct Bible Translation ......... 179
Chapter 3:7 – Who Is God? .................................... 189

## Part Four – YHWH

Chapter 4:1 – The Beginning ................................. 197
Chapter 4:2 – All Things Created Through Him .... 201
Chapter 4:3 – The Beginning of God's Creation .... 209
Chapter 4:4 – GOD, God, or god? ........................... 213
Chapter 4:5 – The Trinity ....................................... 217
Chapter 4:6 – Trinitarian vs. Unitarian .................. 223
Chapter 4:7 – Christ Jesus Rules ............................ 227

Index ......................................................................... 231

# Preface

*The Final Kingdom* is a lifelong endeavor, encompassing more than thirty years of research in scholastic theology. As an ordained minister for more than twenty years, my goal has been to search out concepts in biblical texts without concern for denominational identity or divisions of understanding that all too often segment an otherwise singular faith among Christians. I hold that salvation is through faith in Christ Jesus, while divisive interpretations contradict our Lord's commission to gather unto Him.

Completing this work has included studies in the originally transcribed languages of Hebrew, Greek, and Aramaic, emphasizing ancient history from the beginning of creation itself down through all time since.

I have administered several websites and forums throughout the years, where accomplished expositors of historical texts engage in the common goal of uncovering truths of God's inspired Word. Within these sites, I have presented countless journal articles that I hope have furthered the understanding of God's Word, not only for the benefit of fellow believers but also, by the grace of God, for many new ones, whether online or through my in-person ministry.

# Introduction

This book is written not only to those who have already dedicated their lives in the service of God's kingdom, but to all humanity as well. Every reader, regardless of their level of study of the ancient texts, will find enlightenment within these pages.

The Bible connects and defines itself to uncover God's truths without the need for denominational interpretation to comprehend its message. Unless one understands precisely how the Bible interprets itself, one will never understand the contexts within. It is the continuity of concepts within Scripture we must aspire to identify, rather than any blind acceptance of tradition (Acts 17:11). This work was compiled without denominational identity as a call to all Christians to come together under their common faith in Christ Jesus (Hebrews 10:25).

I hope that this book serves as a sacrifice of praise, bringing God's kingdom message before as many souls as possible (Matthew 28:19–20). Contained within the pages of this work is the very proof of God Himself, and it is time to share this with the world!

May your God, whom you serve continually,
rescue you! (Daniel 6:16)

# Part One
# *Salvation*

Chapter 1:1

# Struggles, Trials, and Strife

W hy is there so much suffering in the world, so much pain? How does one justify humanity's struggles and the strife we all deal with in our everyday lives? All too often, why are we our own worst enemy, punishing ourselves for mistakes we've made or regrets we have? Is there any way we can live life content, with peace of mind, body, and soul?

There is a way to inner peace, the calming of one's mind and spirit, and the assurance of our forgiveness of sin from God. Even if we may at times feel unworthy, we will discover that the only thing keeping us from living a contented life in the service of God's kingdom is our understanding. Who of us did not study a manual before taking a driver's test? Is it likely a new driver will pass such a test without first preparing through careful study of the material involved? If we fail to understand the steps to achieve an objective, then we may find ourselves making mistakes or even failing to pass the test at all. It has been said, "Knowledge is power."

Throughout the pages of the Bible, we have everything we need to learn about why people suffer and why we struggle even when our greatest desire is to serve God. We will discover that our loving Father preserved for us an incredible instructional manual in the Bible to understand why we suffer and how we can obtain contentment within ourselves, despite the trials we all experience. So let's uncover together how we are empowered to take control of our own destinies in the service of God's kingdom.

A form of communication with our heavenly Father that is often overlooked is when He speaks to us outside the Bible's pages. Many people, however, aren't aware of this. The questions we need to ask are: How do we know God is speaking to us personally in our everyday lives? And how do we listen and act in conjunction with that direction from Him?

The answers to these questions are found through obtaining knowledge: first, understanding why there is so much pain and suffering in the world, and second, recognizing how our loving Father speaks to us when there is no clear direction from Scripture. Gaining this knowledge will help us to be more contented in our everyday Christian lives. "Now godliness with contentment is great gain" (1 Timothy 6:6).

The best way to approach this subject is to speak through my own experience and share with you some of the epiphanies and discoveries throughout my journey in the service of God's kingdom. We all have struggles, trials, and strife in life, and we all suffer in our own ways. Yet many of us still desire to serve God in the way He wills for us, despite any hardships we might face. But that journey of serving God as we wish is not always an easy one. Often, our paths are littered with years of mistakes and trials by fire before ever coming to any semblance of spiritual maturity. And since I happen to be one who, unfortunately, has had to learn by experience, let me share a bit of my arduous journey with you.

There are times when I have felt as though I was stuck in a bog, in a pool of quicksand, and with every movement I made, I became ever more stuck, ever more exhausted from struggling. It felt as though this bog was in the center of a battlefield, between two opposing armies, with blood and death all around. I thought that if I just isolated myself from everyone or slept the day away, maybe time would pass me by and leave that pain behind me. But all too often, there was no bottom to that quicksand, no limit or hiding place from the suffering inflicted upon me. I've had loved ones leave us, and experienced illness to the edge of death and poverty without the simplest necessities of life. I have been so stuck in that mire that there seemed no escape, as the battle continually surrounded me, each and every day.

I have also felt as the Apostle Paul did when at times it was my own mistakes and regrets that caused my suffering. "What I wish to do I do not do, but what I do not wish is what I do" (Romans 7:15). I have struggled with addictions as well as my own imperfections and shortcomings. I have made mistakes and bad decisions, and I have made choices based on what I believed our Lord would wish me to do, only to have them fail miserably.

But through all of this pain and hurt, through the mistakes and regret and all the destruction, there was always one constant. Despite anything I suffered, by my own hand or through others, the one thing I have always wanted was to serve God's kingdom appropriately, as He would wish me to. That one singular intent has never left me, and from that consistent seed of hope I have been saved, not only spiritually but physically as well through our Lord, to accomplish great things through service to His kingdom. Regardless of what life throws at you, dear reader, persevere, persist in your dedication, and never let go of that hope in Christ. "I can do all this through him who gives me strength" (Philippians 4:13).

As I have matured through my years in the study of God's Word and lessons by fire, I have learned a few things about the suffering of Christians in a world so opposed to anyone finding contentment through our Lord Christ Jesus. And I hope that somehow, some way, these words may find at least one who can find that contentment through Christ without the need to walk the paths I have or experience the suffering that comes from discovering just how deep that bog can be.

Today when struggles, trials, or strife come my way, the first thing that comes to mind is a question: What would Jesus have done in times like these? I believe that answer is pretty evident: He would have prayed. "Watch and pray so that you will not fall into temptation. The spirit is willing, but the flesh is weak" (Matthew 26:41).

In this regard, let me share one of the most significant changes I have made in my everyday service of God's kingdom that may assist you in your walk in faith. I'm sure you've had those moments when you pray at night in bed before falling asleep. What happens? Your prayers are short because you are tired or don't finish your prayer at all because you fall asleep and regret it the next morning. That experience is one all Christians can relate to, and many may not even realize just how important that feeling of regret is in their desire to make constructive changes in their lives in accord with God's will. Regret can be a powerful gift if we only know how to respond to it.

In response to my desire to better focus my service to God's kingdom, one day I decided to dedicate a room in my home that I could go to in privacy at any time of day, and I would devote that time to prayer when I was fully awake and could apply my full attention. This is undoubtedly one of the most significant changes I have ever made in my dedication to God. I would highly recommend that you consider taking such an action if you have found yourself in prayer when you could not offer your full attention. When I made this commitment to dedicate my full attention to prayer, I discovered that not only was I able to express myself more clearly and concisely, but I also felt as though I was closer to our Lord in those moments. Think about it: How much attention do you think we would get from our loved ones if the only time we spoke to them was when we were half asleep?

Often I have found that many of my struggles and trials are of my own making. From the choices I have made, to the consequences of actions I have taken, the regrets that all too often plagued me came down to the neglect of my heart's greatest desire—to serve God in the manner I wished. Not least are the thorns in my flesh, which are ever present through inherited sin (Romans 5:12). Though we have adopted this sinful condition down through our first parents Adam and Eve, I endeavor to remember our Lord's words when I feel living a godly life seems impossible: nothing is impossible with God! "With man this is impossible, but with God all things are possible" (Matthew 19:26).

> Who shall separate us from the love of Christ? Shall trouble or hardship or persecution or famine or nakedness or danger or sword? As it is written: "For your sake we face death all day long; we are considered as sheep to be slaughtered." No, in all these things we are

more than conquerors through him who loved us. For I am convinced that neither death nor life, neither angels nor demons, neither the present nor the future, nor any powers, neither height nor depth, nor anything else in all creation, will be able to separate us from the love of God that is in Christ Jesus our Lord. (Romans 8:31–39)

Chapter 1:2

# What Is Sin?

What is inherited sin? What is this condition we've all adopted through our genealogy really about? "Therefore, just as sin entered the world through one man, and death through sin, and in this way death came to all people, because all sinned" (Romans 5:12). How can we have a close relationship with our Creator, despite our mistakes and imperfections? Will we ever be able to accept that we are worthy of His forgiveness? Have you asked some of these very questions? If you have, you are not alone, dear reader. Through our walk in service of God's kingdom, we traverse a sinful world constantly bent on drawing us away from our close relationship with our Father. But keep strong in your faith, friends, and know you are not alone; we are a worldwide family! "Be strong and courageous. Do not be afraid; do not be discouraged, for the LORD your God will be with you wherever you go" (Joshua 1:9).

One day I had a conversation about sin and the indulgences of life with a fellow Christian. We discussed whether some pleasures of this world, such as alcohol or activities that could push the limits of decency, were hindrances in our service of God's kingdom. I don't mean to indicate that this brother's opinion was any more lackadaisical than my own, but just that the difference of opinion got me thinking.

The statement from him that stood out the most was, "Personally, I don't think we're approved through personal asceticism or self-denial." What an interesting statement that was. Some may not have paused and considered that comment further, but it sparked a massive debate in my mind; the very first thing I did was look more closely at that word he had used.

> As·cet·i·cism = "Severe self-discipline and avoidance of all forms of indulgence, typically for religious reasons."

He is right on the surface of it; our fasting does not save us from overindulgence; we are saved by grace alone. Yet it must be noted that it is by our actions that our faith is manifest. "In the same way, faith by itself, if it is not accompanied by action, is dead" (James 2:17). How do we understand that by our faith we are saved, but without action that faith is dead? And how do we clarify these two facts within ourselves?

Next I thought of individuals throughout biblical history, such as Noah, Moses, Jonah, and John the Baptist. Noah was a faithful man, but far from perfect. It's indicated in Scripture that he probably at times drank too much and found himself in compromising positions he should not have been in. Moses lived his early life as an Egyptian prince before killing a man and fleeing into the wilderness. Jonah in no way wanted to go to Nineveh, even defying God to begin with, but in the end, he did. Why? John the Baptist ate no delicacies, nor drank wine, but lived on locusts and wild honey in the wilderness and was denoted by our Lord as the greatest man to be born of women. Why did John live a life of asceticism in such a way that many others didn't, wouldn't have, or perhaps in many cases even were expected to? The answers to these questions are, I believe, the answers to how we can live our lives in service to God with clear consciences.

The sacrifice of our fleshly desire is part of our service in God's kingdom; otherwise, there would be no such thing as sin. If we were to disregard the Bible's clear direction on conduct, we would do whatever our fleshly desires deemed appropriate; however, we know this is not proper etiquette for a Christian in service of God's kingdom. Yet one could also take the other extreme and live a life of complete physical asceticism. What is appropriate, and how should we live in accord with God's will?

We should first understand there is clear-cut information from God's Word as to what makes up sin, but also that there are gray areas where personal judgment must come into play. However, it is often within these gray areas we find the most difficulty in serving God's kingdom with a clear conscience. Just as often, it is within these gray areas we learn what inherited sin really is.

The four faithful men I mentioned all had similar circumstances that led to their choices in service of God's kingdom. While Noah and Moses directly spoke to God, their faith in His words showed through their actions. Jonah spoke to God directly, and although he feared the outcome of following His direction, in the end he did so and learned a powerful lesson about God's love for all humanity. Even though there is no account of John speaking directly with God (other than his hearing God's voice at our Lord's baptism), his faith was manifested in his privileged work and service, even having a close association with our Lord Himself.

So, we have more in common with John than we do with these others, as our interactions aren't based on direct verbal communication with God, but rather on what we have learned from eyewitness accounts written down in the pages of the Bible. However, in the end, all three of these men's actions were based on their faith in God's words. But the question remains: Why did John lead a life of such sacrifice, while there is no indication that these other faithful men were expected to?

The differing examples of these men bring me to a question about sacrifice or fasting from certain pleasures of life: At what level do we abstain, or refrain from indulgences of this world, to do God's will? Is it our level of service in God's kingdom that is the deciding factor? Is it the level of dedication we set for ourselves? And given that we do not have direct verbal communication with God, how do we determine the correct level of service, or better said, the correct level of asceticism we must live?

It is at this point I am brought back to the conversation I had with this fellow believer about asceticism, and his next statement: "I think that you must let some things go. I mean, what you think is important to fight against may not be what God sees as important, and let God's Spirit fashion you as He sees fit." At this point in our conversation, I started wondering, how do I determine what kinds of entertainment or indulgences of this world are appropriate for me if I desire to serve God's kingdom, and how does this affect my struggle for a clean conscience before Him?

Let me break it down even a little further. Let's think for a moment about other Christians we associate with in our everyday lives, who each face this same dilemma of serving our Father with a clean conscience. Some of these we may consider as very faithful in their dedication to God when we see them living lives free of many vices. Yet others we may associate with who claim the faith may indulge in activities that we choose not to. For example, some may enjoy alcoholic beverages in moderation, while others may feel uneasy about their consumption. So why do some have no crisis of conscience, while others may feel uneasy about certain indulgences?

Herein lies the detail about how God speaks to us outside the guidance presented in the Bible. John the Baptist decided to live a life of fasting from many pleasures because God's Spirit within him directed him and molded him into the style of life he lived so that he could accomplish God's will in the most effective way possible. John was able to listen to that Spirit from God within him in a way that many other faithful men could not, and this allowed him to have such a wonderful privilege in his work before our Lord. It was by John's acceptance of his role in God's kingdom, and by his following that Spirit within him, that he was spoken of so well by our Lord Christ Jesus. It wasn't for the fact that John lived a life of such asceticism that he was spoken so well of; it was because of his dedication and service in God's kingdom through that Spirit within him that brought him praise. Our Father's will for John was to live the style of life he did, to fulfill his responsibilities before him in the most effective way possible.

And this leads me to our brother's last statement in my conversation with him. "Perfection isn't attained by working against our fleshly drives, but by letting God's Holy Spirit deaden them; otherwise it's a losing battle."

As I have grown in understanding of God's Word, I have come to learn that when we contemplate gray areas of indulgences or the fasting from them, this is a matter of conscience based on the Spirit of God that resides in us. When we have two faithful brothers discussing the trials they face in their service of God and His kingdom, it appears that it is often the struggle against the Holy Spirit within us that we are fighting or not fighting that brings about many of those trials. The Holy Spirit that resides in us is directing us, molding us, forging us by fire through our struggles, trials, and strife. It is that Spirit of God that drives our consciences, that inner voice telling us we are on the right path, or we need to adjust in accord with God's will for us. Outside the pages of the Bible, this is how God speaks to us and directs us to determine whether our actions are glorifying His name or hindering our service to Him. It is that inner voice from God leading us into the service He wills for us. "The Spirit himself testifies with our spirit that we are God's children" (Romans 8:16).

Suppose we wish to serve God's kingdom more than anything in this world and occasionally enjoy a glass of wine while having no conflicts in our relationship with our Father. In that case, we are following that direction given us through His Spirit to enjoy God's gifts of life. If, however, when we drink, we feel as though such actions affect our relationship with Him in a negative way, then that also is God's Spirit speaking to us. Should we not perhaps abstain from those things that stand in the way of our goal to have a more fulfilling service in His kingdom?

This principle can be applied to all aspects of our lives; anything we digest, be it entertainments such as movies, music, whatever it might be, can impact our consciences in service of God's kingdom. We need to learn to listen to that Spirit within us from our Father to serve Him in the capacity He wishes and accomplish His will for us in His kingdom. To some, a particular activity or entertainment form may not be a hindrance, but it may very well be to another. It is this inner voice from God's Spirit we must allow to mold our personalities and help us make necessary adjustments in our day-to-day lives. In so doing, we will start to discover that life of contentment, that calming spirit and clean conscience in our service of God's kingdom.

When we make specific conscientious changes in our everyday lives, such as prayer uninterrupted, abstaining from things that hinder our service of God's kingdom, or simply letting go of the guilt that keeps us from accepting God's forgiveness, we will grow closer to Him. And in so doing, we become of assistance to others in helping them become closer to our heavenly Father as well.

> As for you, the anointing you received from him remains in you, and you do not need anyone to teach you. But as his anointing teaches you about all things and as that anointing is real, not counterfeit—just as it has taught you, remain in him. (1 John 2:27)

I can do all this through him who gives me strength. (Philippians 4:13)

Chapter 1:3

# Trees of the Garden

One evening as I lay in bed, I began to contemplate why we sin and the nature of disobedience against God's commands. I began to consider the very first sin and the events that transpired in the Garden of Eden that led up to Eve disobeying God's direction. What was the nature of Eve's disobedience to God? Was it merely a matter of the fruit looking appetizing, or was there more to her reasoning that ultimately concluded with her sin?

There were two trees of particular note in the garden. One was the Tree of Life and the other the Tree of the Knowledge of Good and Evil. "The LORD God made all kinds of trees grow out of the ground—trees that were pleasing to the eye and good for food. In the middle of the garden were the tree of life and the tree of the knowledge of good and evil" (Genesis 2:9).

God commanded that Adam and Eve might eat from every tree in the garden, except one. "But you must not eat from the tree of the knowledge of good and evil, for when you eat from it you will certainly die" (Genesis 2:17).

Next, a deluding influence the Bible refers to as the liar and the father of lies is introduced into the narrative (John 8:44). Also known as Satan, this angel used a serpent as a mouthpiece to address Eve and question her about God's command to not eat from the Tree of the Knowledge of Good and Evil. "Now the serpent was more crafty than any of the wild animals the LORD God had made. He said to the woman, 'Did God really say, "You must not eat from any tree in the garden?"'" (Genesis 3:1).

This question was chosen as a setup to get to the ultimate purpose of addressing her. "You will not certainly die," the serpent said to the woman. "For God knows that when you eat from it your eyes will be opened, and you will be like God, knowing good and evil" (Genesis 3:4–5).

Now here's the thing: Satan never approached the subject of the fruit being of suitable nourishment to her body, but rather his approach was an attempt to draw out a fleshly desire similar to his own. "You said in your heart, 'I will ascend to the heavens; I will raise my throne above the stars of God; I will sit enthroned on the mount of assembly, on the utmost heights of Mount Zaphon. I will ascend above the tops of the clouds; I will make myself like the Most High'" (Isaiah 14:13–14).

Therefore, when Eve looked at the tree as desirable, her desire was not solely based on the fruit looking flavorful; but instead, she contemplated being like God, knowing good and evil. In this way, Satan presented the idea that somehow God was holding something back from her, that she was missing out on obtaining wisdom God was selfishly denying her.

The text of Genesis informs us that after she contemplated these assertions from the serpent, she developed a longing to fulfill her fleshly desire and then acted on that impulse. "When the woman saw that the fruit of the tree was good for food and pleasing to the eye, and also desirable for gaining wisdom, she took some and ate it" (Genesis 3:6).

This first instance of sin among mankind is an example of what we all deal with now on a daily basis. Sin is going against God's command in order to fulfill selfish desires contrary to His direction. We feel as though we are missing out on something, and we convince ourselves that there is no harm in indulging our flesh, and then when we give in to sin, we find ourselves in violation of our Lord's direction of living a dedicated life.

Today, some six thousand years later, we are all faced with this same dilemma of either following God's direction or giving in to our fleshly desires. So what is at stake? What is at stake is eternal life in new heavens and a new earth!

> Then I saw "a new heaven and a new earth," for the first heaven and the first earth had passed away, and there was no longer any sea. I saw the Holy City, the new Jerusalem, coming down out of heaven from God, prepared as a bride beautifully dressed for her husband. And I heard a loud voice from the throne saying, "Look! God's dwelling place is now among the people, and he will dwell with them. They will be his people, and God himself will be with them and be their God. 'He will wipe every tear from their eyes. There will be no more death' or mourning or crying or pain, for the old order of things has passed away." (Revelation 21:1–4)

How do we sacrifice our desires of the flesh when they contradict clear direction from the pages of the Bible? Knowledge and the fear of our Lord is the beginning of all wisdom. "The fear of the LORD is the beginning of wisdom, and knowledge of the Holy One is understanding" (Proverbs 9:10). Yes, through knowledge, we can fear the consequences of going against God's commands; but the ultimate point is, we respect our Lord as a child does his parents and choose not to sin because He deserves our devotion. Our Father always has our best interests in mind and wishes all mankind to know and love Him and be loved by Him. In 2 Peter 3:9 we read, "The Lord is not slow in keeping his promise, as some understand slowness. Instead he is patient with you, not wanting anyone to perish, but everyone to come to repentance."

Abstaining from fleshly desire is not easy and sometimes can cause heartache within ourselves and others. But know this—your suffering for good will bring about something glorious. When you choose to suffer in your flesh to do God's will, you are proving your faith and ensuring your entrance into eternal life! "Because we know that suffering produces perseverance; perseverance, character; and character, hope" (Romans 5:3–4).

Knowledge is an essential tool in living a godly life and understanding our Father and His right to rule. As an example, let us examine that Tree of the Knowledge of Good and Evil a little closer. That tree represented separation from God. Just as in our universe, there is no such thing as cold, but rather a lack of heat, so also is evil the absence of God. Cold is nothing; it simply does not exist. Therefore, in like manner, sin is nothing, and evil is nothing. Both are simply the absence of God. One day there will no longer be any absence from God, no longer any sin, any evil, or death.

So which do we choose, the path that leads us away from God or the way to eternal life? "He will wipe every tear from their eyes. There will be no more death or mourning or crying or pain, for the old order of things has passed away" (Revelation 21:4).

## The Final Kingdom

We will either choose to live by our own standards of living or our Creator's standards set out within the pages of the Bible. Do we wish to be out in the cold and dark, absent from our Father, or do we wish to be forever in His light, in the warmth of His love, living a perfect life when sin and death are no longer?

> Then the angel showed me the river of the water of life, as clear as crystal, flowing from the throne of God and of the Lamb down the middle of the great street of the city. On each side of the river stood the tree of life, bearing twelve crops of fruit, yielding its fruit every month. And the leaves of the tree are for the healing of the nations. No longer will there be any curse. The throne of God and of the Lamb will be in the city, and his servants will serve him. They will see his face, and his name will be on their foreheads. There will be no more night. They will not need the light of a lamp or the light of the sun, for the LORD God will give them light. And they will reign for ever and ever. (Revelation 22:1–5)

For the wages of sin is death, but the gift of God is eternal life in Christ Jesus our Lord. (Romans 6:23)

Chapter 1:4

# Why We Suffer

Why do we suffer, and why is there so much evil in the world? We may even ask ourselves, why does God allow such suffering to continue? These questions can confuse us and may even dishearten us when faced with the trials of life. However, within the Bible's pages, we learn how sin entered this world and why it has been allowed to continue to our day. Through this study, we will gain the knowledge that empowers us to overcome those moments of confusion or sadness.

When Satan approached Eve in the Garden of Eden, he presented her with a question as to whether God had the authority to dictate right and wrong to His Creation. In essence, Satan was questioning God's right to rule over that which He had created.

After Satan, Adam, and Eve had sinned, God could have destroyed them all and started afresh had He wished to; however, He chose not to. Why? To begin with, the answer to Satan's questioning of God's right to rule would have remained. Satan proposed that mankind could decide right and wrong on their own, governing themselves separate from God's commands. He defiantly suggested that humanity didn't need God's rule at all and they could decide on their own how they should live.

Now that would have presented a problem for those angels alongside God in heaven and any further conscious beings created. Had God destroyed those sinners, the remaining faithful angels in heaven would have been obeying God simply because He said so, rather than providing a constructive example of why God's rule is most beneficial to those He creates. After all, up until this point, there was no such thing as sin or absence from God; therefore, would the question arise again in some future time whether those God created could decide right and wrong for themselves?

Another consequence that would have followed had God destroyed those first sinners would be that Adam and Eve would not have had any children. Consequently, no one who has ever lived would have had the opportunity for eternal life. Through God's choice to allow mankind to govern themselves, not only has He overwhelmingly answered the question of His right to rule, but billions of people have been born and either have or will have the opportunity to learn of their Creator. So in this way, God's love was shown toward those He created in allowing sin and death to enter the human condition, even though Scripture tells us our heavenly Father grieves over the sinful nature of those He created (Genesis 6:6). We suffer because God loved mankind so much that He allowed the future children of Adam and Eve the opportunity to know Him and gain eternal life.

Adam and Eve chose to disobey God, and we inherited this condition from them. But the few years we live with suffering in this world will not compare to life forever with Him, for these former things will not even be remembered or come into our minds at all. "See, I will create new heavens and a new earth. The former things will not be remembered, nor will they come to mind" (Isaiah 65:17).

Our Father so loved the world, He even sent His only begotten Son to die an unwarranted brutal death on behalf of humanity. "For God so loved the world that he gave his one and only Son, that whoever believes in him shall not perish but have eternal life" (John 3:16). We should keep this in mind when we think of how God feels about us. I cannot even imagine what it would have been like to be in such a situation as Abraham's potential sacrifice of Isaac. Our Father was willing to sacrifice His own Son to save countless other lives. That is how much God loves you!

This question of God's right to rule has been settled. Sufficient time has been given to humankind to determine whether they could govern themselves, separate from God's rule. What has been the result? Man rules man to his own detriment. Greed and inequality permeate this world as suffering and hardships continue. "All this I saw, as I applied my mind to everything done under the sun. There is a time when a man lords it over others to his own hurt" (Ecclesiastes 8:9).

One day, I was having a discussion with my young son of seven years about the dangers of the internet. His school had just started issuing tablets in its curriculum to further their education. The students had access to the internet in a limited capacity through software filters, as well as the teacher being able to monitor their accessed material throughout the day on a separate primary device. A fellow student of his was able to access a video online that depicted a written conversation between two seemingly young students. This video targeting young readers was written as if two students communicated during school hours in differing classrooms through text messages.

The narrative began with much of what young ones would discuss, such as trivial matters of fun and games. At which point, one of the characters said they heard loud noises and went on to exclaim that they believed them to be gunshots. The conversation depicted an account of a school shooting, with descriptions of violence and death. Apparently, the ability to access such material had gone unnoticed by their teacher.

Unaware that our son had accessed this material that day, that evening we said our prayers and put him to bed as usual, but less than an hour later, he came to his mother exclaiming he could not sleep. At which point, he told us he was unable to sleep because he kept worrying about the two students he saw on this video online in school. You see, he was unaware that this video was satire, a fictitious depiction created as some demented entertainment.

Needless to say, I was outraged that such a thing was able to be accessed at an institution of learning we rely on to educate and protect our young ones on a daily basis. The principal and teacher were both apologetic and assured us that such an incident would not occur again; but this experience highlights the dangers our young ones face from access to the internet and how they are best served when we regulate that access.

However, during our further conversation about the dangers of the internet, our son made a statement that I will never forget. He did not understand why we regulate his access and time online when all he was interested in was looking up dinosaurs and animals; you see, he wants to be an archaeologist when he grows up. At which point, we engaged in a discussion of the dangers the internet can pose and how access to it can not only be a source of learning and education, but it also contains many hazards that we must protect ourselves from.

It was at that moment our young son made his unforgettable statement. In a sad, down-hearted, heartfelt tone, he exclaimed, "Why does there have to be so much bad in the world?" My heart sank, and to this day it still gets to me; even as I write this, I can still hear his words as I did on the day he said them.

I tried my best to remind him that this condition on earth would not always be as it is now. We explained to him that our regulation and monitoring of his internet access were out of love and our desire for him to have the best opportunity to grow and learn without many of the hardships that can befall us all at a young age. Of course, we cannot shield our young ones from the ugliness of the world; however, we strive to give our children an environment conducive to allowing them to be better equipped to understand the dangers in the world before they need to face them on their own.

We are assured of a time when our Lord's kingdom will come to put an end to suffering and once again rule Creation with love and peace among all humanity, where we may thrive and grow for all eternity.

> In the time of those kings, the God of heaven will set up a kingdom that will never be destroyed, nor will it be left to another people. It will crush all those kingdoms and bring them to an end, but it will itself endure forever. (Daniel 2:44)

The righteous will inherit the land and dwell in it forever. (Psalm 37:29)

Chapter 1:5

# The Image of God

When Christ Jesus began His earthly ministry, He served as an exemplar of what it meant to rule, as the image of God. "The Son is the image of the invisible God, the firstborn over all creation" (Colossians 1:15). Through that example of ruling, He showed us just how we should live. "Whoever claims to live in him must live as Jesus did" (1 John 2:6).

Mankind initially was created in the image of God. "So God created mankind in his own image, in the image of God he created them; male and female he created them" (Genesis 1:27). But what does it mean to be created in the image of God, and what does our Lord's example of being the image of Him teach us about how we should live?

After God created both Adam and Eve, He placed them in the garden, giving them a command to subdue the earth and rule over all living creatures. "God blessed them and said to them, 'Be fruitful and increase in number; fill the earth and subdue it. Rule over the fish in the sea and the birds in the sky and over every living creature that moves on the ground'" (Genesis 1:28). This commission from God was intended for humankind to assist and help all Creation thrive and prosper by extending that garden into all the surrounding world.

However, after Adam and Eve disobeyed God, they were subsequently tossed out of that garden and lost their position of ruling Creation for themselves and their children. In fact, from that day forward, not only were they not to rule in God's image, but they would also alternatively have to toil for their food and indeed protect themselves from wild beasts of the field. "To Adam he said, 'Because you listened to your wife and ate fruit from the tree about which I commanded you, "You must not eat from it," Cursed is the ground because of you; through painful toil you will eat food from it all the days of your life'" (Genesis 3:17).

Through Adam and Eve's fall, we learn that the Tree of the Knowledge of Good and Evil represented a selfish manner of life, where one focuses on their accumulations and greed, rather than being an example of God's way of rule. In effect, deciding right and wrong for oneself is the very definition of sin—the outcome of which is being separated from God Himself.

In contrast, we learn from our Lord's example how Adam and Eve were to originally rule in the image of God. His way of ruling is exemplified by many instances recorded for us throughout Scripture, such as His washing the feet of His disciples, healing the sick, and reaching hearts and minds with the truth of God's Word. As our exemplar, Christ Jesus ruled by assisting others, ultimately showing His greatest sacrifice in love, by offering His life on behalf of all others.

Being in the image of God means assisting and helping others. By following our Lord's example of putting others first in our own lives today, we show ourselves to be living as we were originally intended, in the image of God.

As a far cry from our Lord's example, Satan, Adam, and Eve chose to follow their own desires and fulfill their own selfish wishes in contradiction to God's way of rule. In effect, they decided to worship their own images rather than that of their Creator. Subsequently, mankind down through the ages has suffered the consequences of that choice. However, we are assured that, despite our first parents' disobedience, God's kingdom is to come, restoring all things. "The time has come," he said. "The kingdom of God has come near. Repent and believe the good news!" (Mark 1:15).

God is life and gives His infinite life to others to enjoy Creation as well. God is love, while evil is nothingness, the very absence of God Himself. Nothing will be without Him; yet He will always be. Therefore, the final summation is: The image of God is love, and love is eternal (1 John 4:8).

## The Final Kingdom

Contained within the first prophecy of the Bible is God's means by which He intends to bring about His everlasting kingdom. "And I will put enmity between you and the woman, and between your offspring and hers; he will crush your head, and you will strike his heel" (Genesis 3:15). The striking of our Lord's heel was a minor blow, for through His sacrifice, He accomplished God's will in bringing about a path to righteousness for all mankind. In so doing, He sealed the fate of that original serpent, which will culminate in his being thrown into the lake of fire, a crushing final head blow indeed! (Revelation 20:10).

Our Father, giving over His example of rulership to His Son, returns all life to the way of rule that He originally intended. God's plan for mankind has never changed; He created this world with a purpose and not for nothing. Our first parents' choice to circumvent our Father's command has never affected His original goal for our creation; for humanity will once again return to perfection, no longer living in accord with their own desires but instead living in God's image, in harmony with all Creation. This world's selfish desires will pass away, but God's kingdom will stand forever.

> The world and its desires pass away, but whoever does the will of God lives forever. (1 John 2:17)

I have set you an example that you should do as I have done for you. (John 15:13)

Chapter 1:6

# What Is Salvation?

What is the path to salvation, and how does one obtain it? Are there things we must do to receive salvation? Is faith in our Lord all that is needed to become part of His new kingdom? No doubt, many of us have contemplated these very questions on any number of occasions. Is there a clear-cut answer as to what exactly is required to receive salvation from our Lord and to enter His Final Kingdom?

Let us consider for a moment a conversation between our Lord and a certain young man when he approached Jesus to question Him about the nature of salvation. "Just then a man came up to Jesus and asked, 'Teacher, what good thing must I do to get eternal life?'" (Matthew 19:16).

This gentleman approached Jesus to question Him about what was needed to enter God's kingdom. Our Lord's response, however, was clear and concise, "If you want to enter life, keep the commandments" (Matthew 19:17).

After which, the man went on to question Him further as to what more precisely he must do to gain everlasting life, "Which ones?" (Matthew 19:18). To which our Lord responded, "You shall not murder, you shall not commit adultery, you shall not steal, you shall not give false testimony, honor your father and mother, and love your neighbor as yourself" (Matthew 19:18–19).

This man thought for a moment, and then upon declaring that he had kept all of God's commands, asked Him further what else is needed. "'All these I have kept,' the young man said. 'What do I still lack?'" (Matthew 19:20). It's possible that this young man's continued questioning of Jesus was an attempt on his part to prove his faith. Or perhaps in some way, he thought he was testing Jesus's knowledge of the Law; however, his persistence allowed our Lord to point out a way in which this gentleman could have a more fulfilling role in God's kingdom. "If you want to be perfect, go, sell your possessions and give to the poor, and you will have treasure in heaven. Then come, follow me" (Matthew 19:21). Imagine that—this young man was given a wonderful opportunity to serve alongside the Lord in ushering in God's kingdom! What was this man's response to Jesus's invitation? "When the young man heard this, he went away sad, because he had great wealth" (Matthew 19:22).

Had he left the subject alone, would Jesus have pointed out his excessive love of material possessions? Does our Lord's declaration show that more is needed than mere faith? This account outlines that age-old debate regarding faith versus works, culminating some five hundred years ago in the Reformation. Justification by faith apart from works was the argument, and whether we are saved by faith alone or by works that prove our faith.

There was nothing inherently evil about the fact that this young man had many possessions; it was merely an offer by our Lord to put away such matters to gain a more fulfilling role in building up treasures in heaven. However, Christ Jesus did tell him that he must obey the laws and commandments set out in God's Word to receive salvation. Therefore, action or inaction plays a role in our service of God's kingdom, where that action may affect our salvation.

A simple question to ask ourselves might be: What if this young man had not kept the commands from God as set out in the Law? Would his faith still have allowed his salvation? We might ask ourselves: Did this question of faith versus works change somehow after our Lord's sacrifice? And what exactly are works?

Let's start with salvation after our Lord became the pathway to forgiveness of sin. Is it faith in our Lord's sacrifice alone that results in our salvation? Can one merely believe Christ Jesus came, died for our sins, and then was raised on the third day in order to be redeemed? What does the Bible tell us? Well, for starters, the fallen angels believe. "You believe that there is one God. Good! Even the demons believe that and shudder" (James 2:19). That is all well and good, but what about sinful humans who have the prospect of forgiveness of sin through faith in Christ? One may have faith, but that does not mean one will act in accord with God's commands. Can one have faith but also determine for themselves good and evil, and yet still enter God's kingdom? "The acts of the flesh are obvious: sexual immorality, impurity, and debauchery; idolatry and witchcraft; hatred, discord, jealousy, fits of rage, selfish ambition, dissensions, factions, and envy; drunkenness, orgies, and the like. I warn you, as I did before, that those who live like this will not inherit the kingdom of God" (Galatians 5:19–21).

So, we know that faith alone does not bring us in line with salvation in the presence of gross sin.

> Not everyone who says to me, "Lord, Lord," will enter the kingdom of heaven, but only the one who does the will of my Father who is in heaven. Many will say to me on that day, "Lord, Lord, did we not prophesy in your name and in your name drive out demons and in your name perform many miracles?" Then I will tell them plainly, "I never knew you. Away from me, you evildoers." (Matthew 7:21–23)

Those saying, "Lord, Lord," outlined in Jesus's prophecy not only declared their faith in Him but also even insisted they were doing His works as well. This begs a new question: Can it even be said that faith along with works saves mankind?

First, it should be clear from the very outset that it is by our faith we are justified, and by our confessions we are saved.

> But what does it say? "The word is near you, in your mouth and in your heart" (that is, the word of faith that we proclaim); because, if you confess with your mouth that Jesus is Lord and believe in your heart that God raised him from the dead, you will be saved. For with the heart, one believes and is justified, and with the mouth one confesses and is saved. (Romans 10:8–10, ESV)

So is it merely faith alone that brings us salvation, or is action also needed? It is clear that faith alone without works is dead:

> What good is it, my brothers and sisters, if someone claims to have faith but has no deeds? Can such faith save them? (James 2:14)

> For as the body apart from the spirit is dead, so also faith apart from works is dead. (James 2:26, ESV)

It is at this point we might throw our arms up and exclaim, then who really can be saved? We would not be alone in our confusion, for even Jesus's own disciples had that very same question in response to our Lord's conversation with that young man: "When the disciples heard this, they were greatly astonished and asked, 'Who then can be saved?'" (Matthew 19:25).

However, the path to salvation is quite evident throughout the pages of the Bible and does not need to be a complicated subject. We are empowered through the knowledge of how the Bible explains itself to gain a complete understanding. Scripture is like a painting made up of many brushstrokes. One may stand with their nose to an image, describing each and every brushstroke; however, until one steps back and gets a view of all the brushstrokes together, one will never understand the complete picture. To understand truth, we must comprehensively look at Scripture as a whole, not just a single verse/scripture.

With that in mind, let us look at what the Bible teaches us that is indeed needed to receive eternal life. Firstly, by our faith through our Lord alone, apart from any works, we receive the free gift of life. "For it is by grace you have been saved, through faith—and this is not from yourselves, it is the gift of God" (Ephesians 2:8).

Secondly, we must also understand that we have to obey God's commands to live a moral life as demonstrated by our conduct, regardless of our faith. "Or do you not know that wrongdoers will not inherit the kingdom of God? Do not be deceived: Neither the sexually immoral nor idolaters nor adulterers nor men who have sex with men nor thieves nor the greedy nor drunkards nor slanderers nor swindlers will inherit the kingdom of God" (1 Corinthians 6:9–10).

Lastly, good deeds: Herein lies the whole crux at the very center of what culminated in the Reformation and Martin

Luther's uprising against the oppressive spiritual leaders of his day. Are we expected to offer good deeds on behalf of the free gift of life, in justification of our faith? I invite you to think back to the Garden of Eden: What was the entire focus of the right to rule? Adam and Eve were to rule this world in the image of God but chose instead to circumvent their Father's example by choosing to govern themselves. Rather than offering selfless assistance to others, they selfishly concentrated on their own desires. In contrast, our Lord showed us precisely what God's way of rule is when as the image of Him, He offered His life on behalf of all others.

With that in consideration, what do you think God would like you to do with that free gift of life He gives us through the sacrifice of His Son? Are there examples in Scripture that outline our responsibilities in assisting in the Lord's work? There are. When speaking about the coming of His Father's kingdom, our Lord gave an illustration that outlines His departure and reliance on those He left in charge to continue the work leading up to that kingdom's future arrival.

> Again, it will be like a man going on a journey, who called his servants and entrusted his wealth to them. To one, he gave five bags of gold, to another two bags, and to another one bag, each according to his ability. Then he went on his journey. The man who had received five bags of gold went at once and put his money to work and gained five bags more. So also, the one with two

bags of gold gained two more. But the man who had received one bag went off, dug a hole in the ground and hid his master's money.

After a long time the master of those servants returned and settled accounts with them. The man who had received five bags of gold brought the other five. "Master," he said, "you entrusted me with five bags of gold. See, I have gained five more."

His master replied, "Well done, good and faithful servant! You have been faithful with a few things; I will put you in charge of many things. Come and share your master's happiness!"

The man with two bags of gold also came. "Master," he said, "you entrusted me with two bags of gold; see, I have gained two more."

His master replied, "Well done, good and faithful servant! You have been faithful with a few things; I will put you in charge of many things. Come and share your master's happiness!"

Then the man who had received one bag of gold came. "Master," he said, "I knew that you are a hard man, harvesting where you have not sown and gathering where you have not scattered seed. So I was afraid and went out and hid your gold in the ground. See, here is what belongs to you."

> His master replied, "You wicked, lazy servant! So you knew that I harvest where I have not sown and gather where I have not scattered seed? Well then, you should have put my money on deposit with the bankers, so that when I returned I would have received it back with interest.
>
> "So take the bag of gold from him and give it to the one who has ten bags. For whoever has will be given more, and they will have an abundance. Whoever does not have, even what they have will be taken from them. And throw that worthless servant outside, into the darkness, where there will be weeping and gnashing of teeth." (Matthew 25:14–30)

When our Lord departed this earth after completing all things His Father gave Him to accomplish, He entrusted the work of making disciples into the hands of His followers. Just as in the parable quoted, some have been given many responsibilities, while others few, depending on their abilities. We have a wonderful invitation from our Lord, just as He offered the young man who questioned Him about what it took to gain everlasting life. Either we live as Adam and Eve, concerned more with ruling ourselves, or we can live in the image of God by following our Lord's example of assisting others to learn about His kingdom to come. That may be as simple as discussing God's Word with family members or coworkers or instilling faith in our children. With others, we may have been offered the opportunities to volunteer our time in assisting those in need. In contrast, even further, some have the prospect of spreading the message of God's Word as pastors or preachers.

Whatever our capabilities, we can present ourselves through the example of our Lord to help others obtain that opportunity for everlasting life, as well. And in so doing, we declare our faith in God's way of ruling in any way we are able. "Through Jesus, therefore, let us continually offer to God a sacrifice of praise—the fruit of lips that openly profess his name. And do not forget to do good and to share with others, for with such sacrifices God is pleased" (Hebrews 13:15–16).

Is there any better gift we can offer our fellow humans than to guide them to that same commission we have been given, that of assisting others into eternal life? "Therefore go and make disciples of all nations, baptizing them in the name of the Father and of the Son and of the Holy Spirit" (Matthew 28:19).

Go into all the world and proclaim the gospel to the whole creation. (Mark 16:15)

Chapter 1:7

# The New Creation

Would you choose to live forever if given the opportunity? Some might decline, imagining an eternal life in the world as we see it today. Yet humanity has an inherent desire to live on, to survive; for God has put eternity into our hearts. "He has made everything beautiful in its time. He has also set eternity in the human heart" (Ecclesiastes 3:11).

So if we all share that desire to live on, then why do some brush off the idea of everlasting life? Unfortunately, lack of knowledge has led many to decline the search for eternal life and learning more of their Creator. If someone believes sin and evil will continue forever, they may never even entertain the idea that something much more and much better could be in store for them. The lack of knowledge of what life will be like in the new creation keeps many from learning further about their prospects of entering that eternal kingdom to come. Let us examine what precisely lies before those who long for eternal life in God's kingdom.

We are promised by God that He will bring about a new Creation here on earth and in heaven. The conditions we now see around us will no longer be, and they will never again come into mind. "See, I will create new heavens and a new earth. The former things will not be remembered, nor will they come to mind" (Isaiah 65:17). There will no longer be any sickness or death. "He will wipe every tear from their eyes. There will be no more death or mourning or crying or pain, for the old order of things has passed away" (Revelation 21:4). In this new creation, there will be no more pain, no more struggles or death. Humanity will grow to perfection, where all people will once again obtain what Adam and Eve lost, that one-on-one relationship with God. That is what we have to look forward to, the garden our first parents lost. Mankind will once again rebuild, encompassing all the earth.

We might ask, though: Where is this new creation for mankind to be? Many believe, quite simply, the faithful go to heaven, but is this so?

To begin, many believe our physical planet earth will be destroyed at the battle of Armageddon. Are they right? Let's take a closer look at what the Bible says about the earth itself. "Who laid the foundations of the earth, that it should not be removed forever?" (Psalm 104:5, KJV).

"Generations come and generations go, but the earth remains forever" (Ecclesiastes 1:4). According to Scripture, the earth will stand forever; yet many say that it will be destroyed. This incorrect understanding is derived from their reading of such texts as, "But by the same word the heavens and earth that now exist are stored up for fire, being kept until the day of judgment and destruction of the ungodly" (2 Peter 3:7). However, as I mentioned previously, one cannot look at Scripture like a painting with their nose to it, describing each individual brushstroke. One must step back to describe all brushstrokes as one to comprehend the entire image. The world that will be destroyed at Armageddon is the world of mankind that we see around us now, its sin and death and manner of rule (1 John 2:17). The physical earth, and God's purpose for it, have never changed. Humanity will exist on this planet, just as Adam and Eve were intended to, forever.

It is not the earth itself that has sinned, and our Father did not create it for nothing. "For this is what the LORD says—he who created the heavens, he is God; he who fashioned and made the earth, he founded it; he did not create it to be empty, but formed it to be inhabited—he says: "I am the LORD, and there is no other" (Isaiah 45:18). God created this earth and placed mankind within it to rule in His image. His purpose was for them to live in a perfect world for all eternity, and that purpose has never changed. "But what the LORD has planned will stand forever. His thoughts never change" (Psalm 33:11, CEV).

Some might feel disappointed while reading this, believing they are going to heaven, but it must be noted, we want accurate knowledge of the scriptural text rather than our own understanding, do we not?

If Adam and Eve had not sinned, would they not still be here? Were not mankind and the earth created in perfection, for them to live in complete harmony with God? Was this not His original purpose for this earth and His prophesied intentions for it?

> The righteous will inherit the land and dwell in it forever. (Psalm 37:29)

> A little while, and the wicked will be no more; though you look for them, they will not be found. But the meek will inherit the land and enjoy peace and prosperity. (Psalm 37:10-11)

> But in keeping with his promise we are looking forward to a new heaven and a new earth, where righteousness dwells. (2 Peter 3:13)

> Everyone will sit under their own vine and under their own fig tree, and no one will make them afraid, for the LORD Almighty has spoken. (Micah 4:4)

> The wolf will live with the lamb, the leopard will lie down with the goat, the calf and the lion and the yearling together; and a little child will lead them. The cow will feed with the bear, their young will lie down together, and the lion will eat straw like the ox. The infant will play near the cobra's den, and the young child will put its hand into the viper's nest. They will neither harm nor destroy on all my holy mountain, for the earth will be filled with the knowledge of the LORD as the waters cover the sea. (Isaiah 11:6–9)

Imagine the prospect of being given what Adam and Eve lost: the opportunity to serve in the image of God and fulfill His original purpose by joining our friends and families in cultivating a new garden paradise covering the whole earth! In helping all life grow and prosper, humanity will live in perfect harmony when every tear is wiped away from their eyes (Revelation 21:4). Humankind will be young and beautiful forever, fulfilling all their hearts' desires. "Take delight in the LORD, and he will give you the desires of your heart" (Psalm 37:4).

However, we are told that some of mankind will indeed enter heaven to rule with Christ. "After that, we who are still alive and are left will be caught up together with them in the clouds to meet the Lord in the air. And so we will be with the Lord forever" (1 Thessalonians 4:17). So the questions we may ask are: Who is resurrected to an earthly paradise? And who is destined to rule with Christ in the heavenly kingdom?

## The Final Kingdom

To better understand why some will be raised to heaven, while most will be resurrected to a renewed earth, we can look to John the Baptist as an example, as he is one who will not enter heaven. "Truly I tell you, among those born of women there has not risen anyone greater than John the Baptist; yet whoever is least in the kingdom of heaven is greater than he" (Matthew 11:11). What an interesting verse this is. One who is least of heaven is greater than he. Think about that: John was spoken of as the greatest of men born to women. Yet according to Jesus's words, he is a lesser one than even the least of those in heaven. What does this mean?

John the Baptist missed the new covenant arrangement by reason of his untimely death, when on the evening of Passover, Christ Jesus instituted a new covenant for kingdom rule with His disciples. "In the same way, after the supper he took the cup, saying, 'This cup is the new covenant in my blood, which is poured out for you'" (Luke 22:20). Therefore, through deductive reasoning, if we believe we are going to heaven, are we saying we are greater than John the Baptist?

Would John be missing out on anything by being resurrected to a new earth rather than heaven? No. Think about this: Why did angels before the flood forsake their positions in heaven and come to earth to live as men? Of course, these angels sinned and abandoned their relationship with God; but nonetheless, they envied what mankind had and wanted to have it for themselves. Adam and Eve were created as perfect beings, with a close face-to-face relationship with their Father, and that is a life to be envied. Again, only our perceptions stand in the way of understanding what real life will be like in a paradise earth.

Whether our destiny is to rule as kings with Christ or as most of humanity living within the renewed Garden of Eden, life in the new creations of heaven and earth will be as they initially were created to be, in oneness with God!

See, the stone I have set in front of
Joshua! (Zechariah 3:9)

# Part Two
# Eschatology

Chapter 2:1

# Chronology

The best place to start understanding how the Bible structures the time of the end is Daniel 12:11. Here we find two events separated by a period of 1,290 days. "From the time that the daily sacrifice is abolished and the abomination that causes desolation is set up, there will be 1,290 days" (Daniel 12:11).

Many people believe the daily sacrifice is removed and the abomination set up simultaneously; however, the text and history indicate otherwise. The 1,290 days are the days in between those two events. Although some may believe this text is ambiguous, many translations properly express this prophecy's original intent:

> The daily sacrifice will be stopped. Then, after 1,290 days from that time, a blasphemous object that brings destruction will be set up. (Daniel 12:11, EXB, NCV)

> There will be 1,290 days from the time that the daily sacrifices are stopped, until someone sets up the "Horrible Thing" that causes destruction. (Daniel 12:11, NEV)

> There will be one thousand two hundred ninety days from the time the daily sacrifice is stopped to the setting up of the desolating monstrosity. (Daniel 12:11, CEB)

Often, Scripture presents us with multiple fulfillments of prophecy so that future generations can understand its final fulfillment; it gives us a ruler or gauge, if you will, to better understand how the events spoken of will come to pass. Previous fulfillment of these prophetic events helps us understand the context in which this prophecy was written.

The daily sacrifice in ancient Israel represented the offerings commanded by God to be made by the priests who had charge over the sanctuary. For example, in 66 CE, the temple governor named Eleazar ben Hanania stopped sacrifices for the Roman emperor and Roman people. While considered symbolic, this event was a catalyst that sparked the Jewish revolt, representing a previous fulfillment of the daily sacrifice being removed three and a half years before Rome entered Jerusalem and destroyed the temple.

This prophecy had a previous fulfillment from that of the first century as well. In the Maccabean Revolt of 167–160 BCE, the Seleucid king Antiochus IV Epiphanes set up a statue of his god Zeus within the true God's temple, even sacrificing swine in the sanctuary itself. This was indeed in fulfillment of an abomination within the Holy Place of God's temple.

By these examples, we can say that still yet in the future, the daily sacrifice will be removed 1,290 days before an abomination will be set up within a modern-day fulfillment of this prophetic Holy Place.

The next verse of Daniel is self-explanatory and will help us ground the end-time chronology in a solid concluding point of reference. "Blessed is the one who waits for and reaches the end of the 1,335 days" (Daniel 12:12). The 1,335th day concludes the time periods discussed in Daniel chapter 12, ushering in a blessing for all mankind and marking the first day of the creation of a new earth. "Blessed is the one who will eat at the feast in the kingdom of God" (Luke 14:15).

These 1,335 days are simply an extension of the 1,290 days spoken of in the previous verse. Therefore, both periods of time begin on the same day, while the 1,335th day is 45 days after the 1,290 days end.

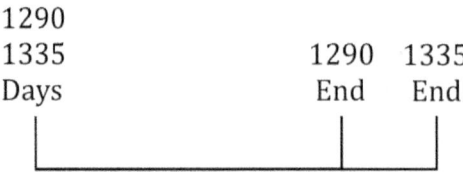

The next place I would like to direct our attention to is Daniel 8:14. "He said to me, 'It will take 2,300 evenings and mornings; then the sanctuary will be reconsecrated'" (Daniel 8:14). These 2,300 evenings and mornings take us back to Genesis's Creation days, where we are told an evening and a morning represent a full day (Genesis 1:5).

The sanctuary set up by God in the wilderness after Israel left Egypt represented heavenly things and acts as a map in understanding the metaphors used within prophecy. (See Chapter 6, The Temple Sanctuary.) The Holy Place was the first room inside the tent itself, housing the showbread, menorah, and incense altar. The Most Holy Place just beyond housed the Ark of the Covenant and represented the very presence of God Himself. While the Holy Place pictured matters pertaining to God's earthly kingdom, the Most Holy Place depicted heaven itself, the very throne of God. So then, when Daniel 8:14 speaks of a time when the sanctuary will be cleansed, it is speaking of the new heaven and new earth. Therefore, the 2,300 days and the 1,335th day both end on the same day, that of the new creation.

Within these 2,300 days, we find a time period when a rebellion of the Lord's people will be visible alongside the daily sacrifice. "Because of rebellion, the LORD's people and the daily sacrifice were given over to it" (Daniel 8:12).

While we've discussed how the daily sacrifices of old represented those at the temple in Jerusalem, today the daily sacrifices are symbolized by a faithful one's declaration in praise to others about the Good News of God's kingdom to come.

> The high priest carries the blood of animals into the Most Holy Place as a sin offering, but the bodies are burned outside the camp. And so, Jesus also suffered outside the city gate to make the people holy through his own blood. Let us, then, go to him outside the camp, bearing the disgrace he bore. For here we do not have an enduring city, but we are looking for the city that is to come. Through Jesus, therefore, let us continually offer to God a sacrifice of praise—the fruit of lips that openly profess his name. And do not forget to do good and to share with others, for with such sacrifices God is pleased. (Hebrews 13:11–16)

Therefore, through Christian praise and preaching delivered to others, the daily sacrifice has its fulfillment in our day.

So then, while all of this befell Jerusalem when Rome surrounded that city before ultimately destroying the temple for the Jewish nation's rebellion against God in the first century, this event also serves as a touchstone for that which is to come. We are told that, as part of these 2,300 evenings and mornings, there will be a rebellion (or apostasy) on the part of His people today, which will culminate in the ceasing of their ability to continue to preach about the coming of God's kingdom.

As a great structural overview, within these 2,300 days, we are given an entire time period that this apostasy, alongside the daily sacrifice, will continue, be removed, then the abomination set up before the sanctuary is cleansed. "'How long will it take for the vision to be fulfilled—the vision concerning the daily sacrifice, the rebellion that causes desolation, the surrender of the sanctuary and the trampling underfoot of the LORD's people?' He said to me, 'It will take 2,300 evenings and mornings; then the sanctuary will be reconsecrated'" (Daniel 8:13–14).

By comparing Daniel chapter 8 with Daniel chapter 12, we recognize a time period between the observance of apostasy on the part of God's people and the daily sacrifice being removed. Since the 1,335 days and the 2,300 days end on the same day, then we can see that the 2,300 days began well before the 1,335 days began.

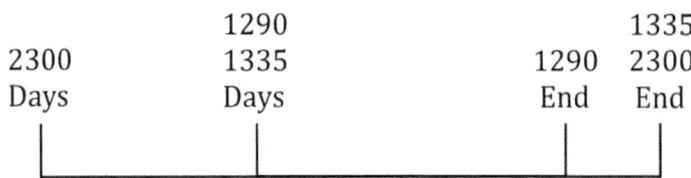

Next, we draw our attention to another time period mentioned in Daniel chapter 12 that furthers our understanding of the time of the end, denoted as the times, time, and half a time. "It will be for a time, times and half a time. When the power of the holy people has been finally broken, all these things will be completed" (Daniel 12:7).

To understand these times, we are directed to the book of Revelation, chapter 12, where we are told exactly how long this period is. "The woman was given the two wings of a great eagle, so that she might fly to the place prepared for her in the wilderness, where she would be taken care of for a time, times and half a time, out of the serpent's reach" (Revelation 12:14). Within this same chapter, this time period is explained as 1,260 days. "The woman fled into the wilderness to a place prepared for her by God, where she might be taken care of for 1,260 days" (Revelation 12:6). Therefore, this time period mentioned in Daniel chapter 12 equals three 360-day biblical years, and one half of a year, or 180 days, for a total of 1,260 days.

This woman mentioned in Revelation chapter 12 is that same woman who is spoken of in the very first prophecy of Genesis 3:15 and represents the true organizational arrangement on earth by God. Therefore, the moment when this woman flees into the wilderness is the moment when the preaching work is ceased. This was also the event that those in Jerusalem would have been looking for, to flee when seeing the daily sacrifices at the temple removed in

## The Final Kingdom

66 CE. "When you see Jerusalem being surrounded by armies, you will know that its desolation is near. Then let those who are in Judea flee to the mountains, let those in the city get out, and let those in the country not enter the city" (Luke 21:20–21).

We also have confirmation of this time period from Revelation chapter 11, where forty-two thirty-day months are mentioned as the time period that the courtyard surrounding the temple is trampled by the Gentiles: "I was given a reed like a measuring rod and was told, 'Go and measure the temple of God and the altar, with its worshipers. But exclude the outer court; do not measure it, because it has been given to the Gentiles. They will trample on the holy city for 42 months. And I will appoint my two witnesses, and they will prophesy for 1,260 days, clothed in sackcloth'" (Revelation 11:1–3).

If we go back to our chronology in Daniel chapter 12, we see that the time, times and half a time, or 1,260 days, begin the moment the daily sacrifice is removed, the same day the 1,290 and 1,335 days begin.

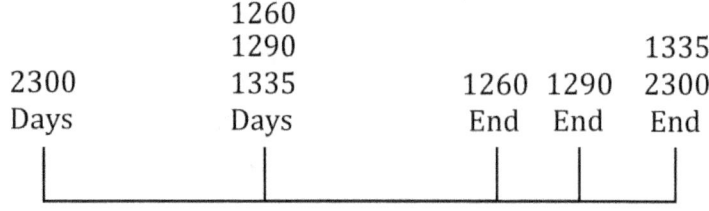

As we arrange the chronology of the time of the end into its proper sequence, we are presented with the structure of events that will one day unfold to usher in God's kingdom. Two thousand three hundred days before the new creation, we see an apostasy on the part of God's people. Then, the modern-day representation of the daily sacrifice is removed, starting the 1,335 days. Subsequently, 1,260 days later, the two witnesses are no longer dressed in sackcloth, a sign of mourning, when the woman is brought out from the wilderness where she had been protected, establishing God's spiritual temple once again on earth. It is this newly established sanctuary in which the abomination is set up thirty days later, at the end of 1,290 days, when that newly rebuilt spiritual temple is attacked.

In some misguided thought process, those coming against God's spiritual temple, in the end, believe they can circumvent the events about to come upon the world. Thinking that if they attack and kill the remaining of God's holy ones on earth, then the Lord will leave this planet and them alone. How mistaken they are. For it is at that moment they will rouse the True God and find their destruction in the battle of Armageddon!

> Why do the nations conspire and the peoples plot in vain? The kings of the earth rise up and the rulers band together against the LORD and against his anointed, saying, "Let us break their chains and throw off their shackles." (Psalm 2:1–3)

For this is what the LORD Almighty says: "After the Glorious One has sent me against the nations that have plundered you—for whoever touches you touches the apple of his eye." (Zechariah 2:8)

As we continue through the chronology of the time of the end, what you are about to discover is the very proof of God Himself! Through this chronology, God has revealed Himself as the only personage who could have established this prophetic structure within the pages of the Bible, spanning down through thousands of years.

It is coming! It will surely take place, declares the Sovereign LORD. (Ezekiel 39:8)

Chapter 2:2

# Holy Days

What I am about to share with you is one of the most extraordinary periods in my study of God's Word and contains the very proof of God Himself. Incorporated throughout the scriptural texts is evidence of a singular writer, spanning more than three thousand years of biblical history. As you continue to study into the subsequent chapters of this work, you will discover just how He accomplished such an awe-inspiring feat to assist us in ushering in His Final Kingdom.

The Lord established holy days as remembrances in the nation of Israel throughout their tumultuous history, as prophetic time markers for the fulfillment of events that would bring about His people's promised deliverance.

These holy days that God commanded the Israelites of old to uphold were set up as appointed fasts or feasts that were to be proclaimed in their appointed times:

> Speak to the people of Israel and say to them, These are the appointed feasts of the LORD that you shall proclaim as holy convocations; they are my appointed feasts. (Leviticus 23:2, ESV)

> These are the LORD's appointed festivals, the sacred assemblies you are to proclaim at their appointed times. (Leviticus 23:4)

Several of these holy days were fulfilled in Christ Jesus Himself, such as the example of Passover, remembered as the evening of the last plague in Egypt, and fulfilled in our Lord when on the very day of its observance, He was sacrificed for the many for the forgiveness of sin (Leviticus 23:5).

Next, unleavened bread was established as a remembrance to point to the prophetic fulfillment of our Lord's perfect, sinless body that He offered on our behalf in fulfillment of that holy remembrance as well (Leviticus 23:6).

Christ Jesus fulfilled firstfruits, representing the first of the harvest brought before the Lord in ancient Israel when He was resurrected on the very day of its observance, just as explained by the Apostle Paul, "But Christ has indeed been raised from the dead, the firstfruits of those who have fallen asleep" (1 Corinthians 15:20; see also Leviticus 23:10).

Our Lord fulfilled Pentecost as His disciples gathered on that observance day when they received the outpouring of the Holy Spirit as a helper in the work to come (Acts 2:3).

Still yet to be fulfilled are the fall holy days of the Feast of Trumpets, Day of Atonement, and Tabernacle. Through these holy days, the appointed times of the end will usher in God's kingdom. "For the revelation awaits an appointed time; it speaks of the end and will not prove false. Though it linger, wait for it; it will certainly come and will not delay" (Habakkuk 2:3).

Our Lord has revealed to us through prophecy that these fall holy days yet to be fulfilled overlay the chronology set out in the book of Daniel precisely and coincide with the very day and context of each of their respective days, in the time of the end.

The Hebrews used a lunisolar calendar. The months were based on the lunar cycle, while the years were based on that of the solar procession. Consequently, a month or a day was added periodically to equalize the lunar calendar with the solar. In so doing, the holy days do not always fall on the same day every year, in conjunction with the Gregorian calendar.

In fact, we find that over 2,300 days, the holy days yet to be fulfilled vary by the number of days in between them, depending on the decades studied. Ultimately, after calculations spanning more than a century before our time and a century still future, there are only a handful of times in each century when these holy days line up with Daniel's chronology.

Let me give you an example: September 10, 2018, marked the first day of Rosh Hashana (Trumpets). Starting from that date and ending 2,300 days later, on December 26, 2024, you come to the holy day of Hanukkah, a remembrance our Lord observed, marking the cleansing of the Holy Place during the Maccabean revolt of 167–160 BCE. Seventy-five days before this, on October 12, 2024, we find the holy day of Yom Kippur (Day of Atonement), which is the day in the end when our Father's spiritual temple is reestablished on earth in completion of the 1,260 days.

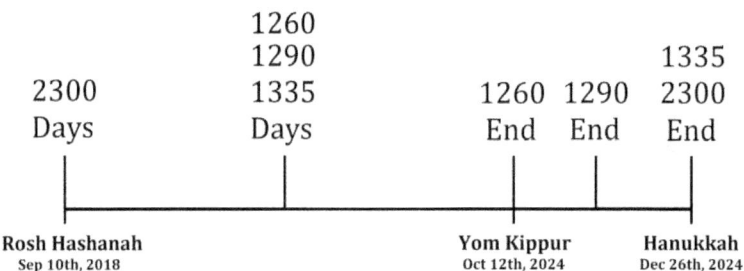

Given that 2018 did not usher in the beginning of the time of the end and the arrival of God's kingdom, using this current structure, one finds that 2029–2035 and 2032–2038 also coincide with the holy days yet to be fulfilled and the chronology set out in the book of Daniel.

Now what about the holy day of Sukkot (Tabernacles)? What about some of the so-called minor fasts remembered by the kingdom of Israel? Do they have any fulfillment and possible alignment with the chronology of the time of the end?

Let's look at another time period mentioned in the book of Daniel: In chapter 7, we have a vision of four fearsome beasts representing a succession of earthly kingdoms. While out of the fourth comes a horn that wages war against the holy people and defeats them, the beast itself is thrown into a fire and burned, denoting its destruction. At this point, the other beasts are spoken of as continuing for a period of time after their ruling power is taken away. "As for the rest of the beasts, their dominion was taken away, but their lives were prolonged for a season and a time" (Daniel 7:12, ESV).

As we learned from Revelation chapter 12, a time equals 360 days. Given that four seasons are in a year, a season marks a fourth of those days (Genesis 8:22). Therefore, when the fourth beast of Daniel chapter 7 is destroyed, the other kingdoms continue on for 450 days. Since these nations are put to their end at the coming of God's kingdom, the end of these other beasts comes at the completion of the 2,300 days, the very day of the new heavens and new earth.

As it just so happens, counting back 450 days from the end of the 2,300 days brings us to the holy days of Sukkot! You see, this was a festival set up by God for His people wandering in the wilderness for forty years as a reminder of their living in a foreign land. How fitting that these holy days fall on the very same day when the kingdoms of this world lose their dominion, when the fourth beast goes into the abyss, and an eighth arises to do battle with the Lord (Leviticus 23:40; Revelation 17:11). It will be at this time that God's people will be living in a foreign land indeed.

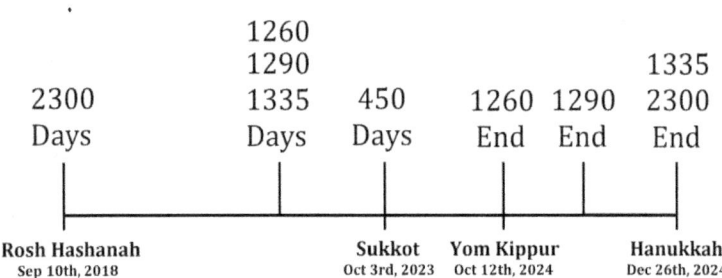

This festival of Sukkot is a seven-day holiday in which the events to unfold in fulfillment of this remembrance could span the entirety of these days; however, it is quite clear that whatever causes the fourth beast's collapse, this event will have world-shattering effects.

In Daniel chapter 11, we read of a "pushing" between the kings of the North and South (Daniel 11:40). In conjunction with the collapse of the fourth beast, this pushing results in war among nations of the world. While it is clear that war will continue from this point on in the time of the end, wars may not always include conventional means (Matthew 24:6). Nations can also take other actions to undermine adversaries, such as bringing low enemies through unconventional warfare. Economic collapse, for example, has many times been a precursor to conflict throughout humanity's history. However, whatever the catalyst that results in this pushing among nations, the outcome will combine all nations into a conglomerate entity in opposition to God's kingdom. "The beast who once was, and now is not, is an eighth king. He belongs to the seven and is going to his destruction" (Revelation 17:11). Not unlike the Tower of Babel of old, the nations coming together under the guise of peace serve their ill-fated goal of advancing against the kingdom of God! "Then they said, 'Come, let us build ourselves a city, with a tower that reaches to the heavens, so that we may make a name for ourselves; otherwise we will be scattered over the face of the whole earth'" (Genesis 11:4).

We now have four holy days that line up with Daniel's chronology on the exact days the events spoken of are to occur. There is, however, much more to come, as our Father's hand continues to be revealed throughout the pages of the Bible, as its singular author. Does not this evidence of our Lord's precision fill you with the Holy Spirit?

Chapter 2:3

# Time of the End

As we continue our look into the chronology of the Bible and how God's holy days coincide with the completion of prophecy, let us examine another prophetic time period mentioned in the book of Daniel. In the fourth chapter, Nebuchadnezzar, king of Babylon, dreamed of a heaven-high tree that provided food and shelter to the most distant parts of the earth. This tree represented the king himself and the vast province he controlled. Daniel explained that Nebuchadnezzar's vision was to show how God was to humble him and proclaimed he was to lose his kingdom for a period of seven times (seven biblical years of 360 days each) for his presumptuousness.

Twelve months later, as Nebuchadnezzar was walking on the roof of his palace, he began to boast about his accomplishments, "Is not this the great Babylon I have built as the royal residence, by my mighty power and for the glory of my majesty!" (Daniel 4:30). It was at this moment when Daniel's proclamation of the vision came true. Nebuchadnezzar lost his sanity and lived among the wild animals of the field until the day he acknowledged the Most High was sovereign over all kingdoms of the earth (Daniel 4:32).

At the end of these seven times, Nebuchadnezzar raised his eyes to heaven, and his sanity was restored to him, as was his kingdom. All of this came to pass to humble the king, just as the explanation of the vision given to Daniel had foretold (Daniel 4:34). The account goes on to tell us that from that day on, Nebuchadnezzar praised and glorified the God of heaven.

What is of considerable note about this account in the fourth chapter of Daniel is a passage that ties this prophetic vision to the time of the end. "This punishment is given at the command of the holy angels. It will show to all who live that God Most High controls all kingdoms and chooses for their rulers persons of humble birth" (Daniel 4:17, CEV).

Far from being a prophetic fulfillment for Nebuchadnezzar alone, this vision is an account for all living, so that these may know that the Most High is sovereign and sets up over the kingdom of the earth whom He pleases. It will be by this vision of the tree in Daniel chapter 4 that the whole world will indeed see who the Most High sets up over the kingdom of the earth.

This tree is said to be cut down for a period of seven times. From our understanding of Revelation chapter 12, we know these seven times are made up of 360 days each, making a total of 2,520 days.

There is a moment in the time of the end when we know all mankind will be aware of God's establishing kingship of Christ Jesus over the whole earth, and that is the day our Lord appears in the clouds. "Look, he is coming with the clouds, and every eye will see him, even those who pierced him; and all peoples on earth will mourn because of him. So shall it be! Amen" (Revelation 1:7; see also Mark 13:26).

To understand when this moment occurs in the end, we must go back to Daniel's end-time chronology. In fulfillment of Yom Kippur, Christ Jesus is crowned over the earthly kingdom; yet this is not the moment He appears in the clouds, for there are still many events to be fulfilled before He is revealed to the world. In fact, there are forty days between the ending of the 1,260 days when God's spiritual temple is established on earth to the moment Christ appears in the clouds. In fulfillment of all prophetic accounts of forties throughout Scripture, there will be forty days from the moment our Lord is crowned over the earthly kingdom until His appearance before all mankind. This mirrors our Lord's example after He was resurrected, as He spent forty days on and off with His disciples before being raised to heaven (Acts 1:3). In like manner, at Yom Kippur, the Holy Spirit is to be poured out, Christ's brothers will be transfigured, and then forty days later they will meet Him in the clouds.

Also, in these forty days within the end times is a ten-day period of tribulation for the church in Smyrna (Revelation 2:10), for their tribulation occurs when the abomination is set up after the 1,290 days' end. Therefore, adding ten days of Smyrna's tribulation after the day the abomination is set up brings us to the fortieth day from Yom Kippur and the day our Lord appears in the clouds before all mankind.

If we count back seven times from our Lord's appearance in the clouds, is there anything of significance we can glean from the beginning of this time period? When one counts back 2,520 days before our Lord's appearance, we find another holy day, the very day of Asara B'Tevet! God set up this fast in remembrance of the day Nebuchadnezzar surrounded and laid siege to Jerusalem during the First Temple period, leading up to Jerusalem's destruction and its people being taken captive into Babylon.

On many occasions, our Lord foretold Jerusalem's destruction if they failed to turn around from their sinful ways. Prophets of old link us right back to Nebuchadnezzar's dream through perpetual warnings of Israel's apostasy. From the tree itself providing food and shelter for birds and animals to the iron and copper that tethered the stump, these prophecies of old mirror the removal of the heaven-high tree in the fourth chapter of Daniel:

> I will break down your stubborn pride and make the sky above you like iron and the ground beneath you like bronze. (Leviticus 26:19)

> On the mountain heights of Israel I will plant it; it will produce branches and bear fruit and become a splendid cedar. Birds of every kind will nest in it; they will find shelter in the shade of its branches. (Ezekiel 17:23)

> Its leaves were beautiful, its fruit abundant, and on it was food for all. Under it the wild animals found shelter, and the birds lived in its branches; from it, every creature was fed. (Daniel 4:12)

Here we come to one of the most amazing epiphanies in our study of the timeline of the end. When we add these seven times into our chronology, there is only one time period in the twenty-first century when Asara B'Tevet lines up with Daniel's chronology

# Timeline of the End

(7 Times, 7 Years Begin)
Beginning of the End: December 28, 2028 – Asara B'Tevet
|
(2,300 Days Begin)
Apostasy: September 10, 2029 – Rosh Hashanah
|
(1,260, 1,290, 1,335 Days Begin)
Preaching Given to Babylon: May 2, 2032
|
(450 Days Begin)
State Collapse: October 4, 2034 – Sukkot
|
(1,260 Days End)
Coronation: October 13, 2035 – Yom Kippur
|
(1,290 Days End)
Abomination: November 12, 2035
|
(7 Times End)
Christ Appears: November 22, 2035
|
(7 Years, 2,300, 1,335 Days End)
The Final Kingdom: December 28, 2035 – Hanukkah

Quite literally, if God's kingdom is to be established on earth within this century, December 28, 2028, to December 28, 2035, is the only time period when the holy days yet to be fulfilled line up with the chronology of Daniel in accord with the evidence our Lord has given us throughout the pages of the Bible. On the very same day the temple was cleansed in the second century BCE, so it will be in the future when God's kingdom comes and cleanses this world in fulfillment of that faithful day, Hanukkah!

If you look at the timeline presented on the previous page, we can also note the "7 Years End." If you add the remaining days till the beginning of the new earth from the ending of the 2,520 days, or seven times, you get 2,556 days, and that is precisely a seven-year solar cycle, not a day more, nor a day less! How amazing is the fact that God has included the entire lunisolar process within the time of the end! Only God Himself could have constructed such a prophetic timetable spanning millennia for His people to know just how He plans to usher in His Final Kingdom. Therein lies the very proof of God's authorship of the Holy Bible itself. The odds of these holy days combining with prophecy and matching each event precisely are astronomical. The number is nearly incalculable, given the details that correspond to bringing together this completed timeline. What an amazing example of God's foresight and all-knowing power!

What might we see in this future fulfillment of Asara B'Tevet and the surrounding of God's spiritual temple? It is quite possible that just as with those events from Israel's past, we will see nations declaring new laws in contradiction to pure worship. Suppose we see news reports of governments coming against Christian sensibilities on December 28, 2028, by enacting regulations that violate God's commands. In that case, we will know the beginning of the end is at hand, and our Lord is close at the door (Daniel 7:25). Or it is just as possible that we might see the declaration of wrongdoing or violation of law on the part of God's people in fulfillment of Asara B'Tevet. Whatever the motivation of governments to come against God's people, it will be by their words and narrative that nations will surround them on a worldwide stage.

Whether the events presented here occur on these dates or not plays no part in our worship of the sovereign of the universe. We must keep in mind that our dedication to and faith in the Lord Christ Jesus are not based on possible end-time fulfillment of prophecy, but rather on the Spirit within us from our Lord that allows us the opportunity to serve Him because He deserves our devotion (Revelation 4:11). We serve God's kingdom through our love for Him, as nothing can separate us from that love. "Neither height nor depth, nor anything else in all creation, will be able to separate us from the love of God that is in Christ Jesus our LORD" (Romans 8:39).

Now let us see if there are any other timetables we have not discussed that coincide with this established chronology set out in the book of Daniel. Indeed, there are . . .

Chapter 2:4

# Seventy Weeks

The book of Daniel serves as a watershed of information about the end times as it continues to reveal itself as the very work of God Himself. And there is yet another time period mentioned within that book that will help us understand the chronology of the time of the end.

In the ninth chapter of Daniel, we read of a period of seventy weeks, denoting the ushering in of several events. "Seventy 'sevens' are decreed for your people and your holy city to finish transgression, to put an end to sin, to atone for wickedness, to bring in everlasting righteousness, to seal up vision and prophecy and to anoint the Most Holy Place" (Daniel 9:24).

These seventy weeks concern the apostasy of God's people, culminating in removing the daily sacrifice or preaching work and ultimately the anointing of God's king at the high holy day of Yom Kippur. The consequence of this removing of the preaching work is discipline of God's people before their spiritual temple will be rebuilt when Christ's kingdom is established on earth, ending the sixty-ninth week.

As I mentioned previously, prophecy often depicts multiple future fulfillments so that the additional fulfillments can be understood through past fulfilled examples; and these prophecies of Daniel chapter 9 are no different. There is, however, great debate over the exact year these seventy weeks began before our common era, but as far as the prophecy concerns our day, it doesn't matter when they began, as we will discover here.

Prophecy was recorded for us in God's Word for His people to understand events relating to His kingdom to come. Therefore, whether the Israelites should have been looking for the year twenty-seven, twenty-nine, thirty, or thirty-one for the Mashiach's ("Messiah" in Hebrew) appearance is irrelevant, for the prophecy's fulfillment in our day does not rely on when its first fulfillment began. However, what we do know about this prophecy is all we need to understand the end-time fulfillment of these seventy weeks.

During this prophecy's first fulfillment, from the call to rebuild Jerusalem until the Messiah's appearance was to be sixty-nine weeks. Now, I would like to bring attention to that final seventieth week. "And he shall make a strong covenant with many for one week, and for half of the week he shall put an end to sacrifice and offering. And on the wing of abominations shall come one who makes desolate, until the decreed end is poured out on the desolator" (Daniel 9:27, ESV).

This mention of the "many" is a common expression throughout Scripture to denote the Israelites themselves. The covenant in Daniel 9:27 is the Davidic covenant's promise for the Messiah. The one who confirms that covenant is none other than the Anointed One Himself. This covenant is confirmed through the promised Messiah when Christ Jesus was baptized in the Jordan by John. It was at that moment the Davidic covenant was confirmed for the Israelites for seven years, beginning the seventieth week.

At the half of that week, sacrifice and gift offerings were put to an end. These were the physical sacrifices made at the temple sanctuary for the forgiveness of sin. Once Christ Jesus was cut off at the half of that seventieth week, those sacrifices at the temple were no longer needed nor relevant. At which point the curtain separating the Holy Place from the Most Holy Place was rent in two, allowing access into heaven through Christ Jesus Himself.

Many have believed that the stoning of Stephen played some particular role in the fulfillment of these seventy weeks; however, this thought process does nothing to further our understanding of how this prophecy is to be fulfilled in the time of the end.

However, another event of great significance occurred at about the same time as Stephen's stoning, which does fall in line with the prophesy in Daniel chapter 9, and by it, we gain a complete picture of this seventieth week.

If the covenant for a Messiah was held in place for the Israelites for a period of one week, or seven years, then the logical question is: When was that covenant for the messianic kingdom extended to all mankind?

Cornelius, the centurion, was an Italian officer stationed in Caesarea who had become the first Gentile to have been anointed under the Christian faith. No longer merely for the "many/Israelites," now that covenant arrangement for a messianic kingdom was extended to all mankind at the completion of that seventieth week when Peter baptized Cornelius the centurion and his family.

Our attention today, however, is directed toward this prophecy's fulfillment in the time of the end. These seventy weeks concern rebuilding the spiritual temple on earth after the preaching work has ceased. Ending the sixty-ninth week, Christ Jesus is given rulership over the earthly kingdom, His two witnesses are transfigured, and the covenant for a kingdom is confirmed to God's people.

In congruence with all other day counts of Daniel's prophecies, these weeks in the time of the end will be seventy weeks of seven days each and begin on the 777th day of God's people going into spiritual captivity after the ceasing of the Lord's preaching work. At this moment, a call by the two witnesses goes out to rebuild the spiritual temple on earth in gathering back all His people into true worship under God's kingdom (Ezekiel 37:1–14).

Continued…

# Timeline of the End

(7 Times, 7 Years Begin)
Beginning of the End: December 28, 2028 – Asara B'Tevet

|

(2,300 Days Begin)
Apostasy: September 10, 2029 – Rosh Hashanah

|

(1260, 1290, 1,335 Days Begin)
Preaching Given to Babylon: May 2, 2032

|

(777th Day, 69 Weeks Begin)
Call to Rebuild Jerusalem: June 17, 2034

|

(450 Days Begin)
State Collapse: October 4, 2034 – Sukkot

|

(1,260 End/70th Week Begins)
Coronation: October 13, 2035 – Yom Kippur

|

(1290 End)
Abomination: November 12, 2035

|

(7 Times End)
Christ Appears: November 22, 2035

|

(7 Years, 2,300, 1,335 Days End)
The Final Kingdom: December 28, 2035 – Hanukkah

Mirroring our Lord's experience, His two witnesses are martyred at the halfway point of this seventieth week, then raised before the eyes of the whole world three and a half days later. "For three and a half days some from every people, tribe, language and nation will gaze on their bodies and refuse them burial" (Revelation 11:9). Once God's two witnesses are resurrected in full view of the world, there will be a message from an angel, inviting all humanity into this new kingdom. In just the same way that Cornelius represented the Gentiles of his day, so Christ's covenant for a kingdom will be extended to all mankind at that moment, ending the seventieth week. "Then I saw another angel flying in midair, and he had the eternal gospel to proclaim to those who live on the earth—to every nation, tribe, language, and people. He said in a loud voice, 'Fear God and give him glory, because the hour of his judgment has come. Worship him who made the heavens, the earth, the sea and the springs of water'" (Revelation 14:6–7).

These prophecies of Daniel chapter 9 would have helped the Jewish nation of the first century to identify the coming of the Messiah in the same way these prophecies will help us to identify our Lord's return still yet to come. When we see these things start to unfold, we will know His kingdom is at hand!

> Even so, when you see all these things, you know that it is near, right at the door. (Matthew 24:33)

Chapter 2:5

# The Day or Hour

It is a common belief among Christians that no one could ever know when the end will be, and many will quote Scripture that they believe prove this understanding. If you are one who steadfastly believes no one can ever know when the end will come, I invite you to make sure of all things (1 Thessalonians 5:20–21). Let's take a look:

> But about that day or hour no one knows, not even the angels in heaven, nor the Son, but only the Father. (Mark 13:32)

What did Jesus mean when He said, "day or hour no one knows?" His disciples would have understood; however, this general saying has fallen away from favor over time. He was speaking of the fulfillment of Rosh Hashanah, a two-day holy day in which two witnesses would be entrusted with the work of spotting a new moon, beginning the new year. They were never sure which of the two days it would fall on, hence why the holy day became known as "the day or hour no one knew." He was saying no one knew when Rosh Hashanah's fulfillment would be; but it should also be obvious He was speaking of everyone alive at that moment. His message was present tense and indicates that no one at that time knew when the prophecy of Rosh Hashanah would ultimately be fulfilled, other than God Himself.

Conversely, our Father makes it very clear that the end will not come unless first His prophets know when and how it will come to be. "For the LORD GOD does nothing without revealing his secret to his servants the prophets" (Amos 3:7, ESV). God had always had His faithful prophets on earth to declare His coming judgments before they occurred.

Granted, we do not currently know if that faithful Rosh Hashanah will be fulfilled in our lifetime. But we can be assured that once the end does begin, mankind will know when each event will be fulfilled by the Lord's direction through His two witnesses. Everything God gives us through prophecy is to assist us in being ready for when that time comes; and we are without a doubt instructed to be prepared and on the watch for His day (Luke 21:28).

Now what about Paul's words here? "But you, brothers and sisters, are not in darkness so that this day should surprise you like a thief" (1 Thessalonians 5:4).

Paul explained that the Son of Man coming as a thief was directed toward only the wicked, for he said that Jesus would not come as a thief to the faithful. Paul made it very clear that if you do not wake up and keep watch, the Lord comes upon you as a thief. "Remember, therefore, what you have received and heard; hold it fast, and repent. But if you do not wake up, I will come like a thief, and you will not know at what time I will come to you" (Revelation 3:3). Jesus does not come at an hour you least expect if you keep on the watch. He only comes as a thief to the wicked.

So then, our Lord comes as a thief only to those not expecting Him. The term *thief* is used to denote the taking away of something, and that which is taken away is one's name from the Book of Life. Instead, let us stay awake in our faith, keeping on the watch, so the Lord does not come as a thief unto us; but instead, He knocks and enters to take the evening meal with us. "Here I am! I stand at the door and knock. If anyone hears my voice and opens the door, I will come in and eat with that person, and they with me" (Revelation 3:20).

For, as the wise virgins, His faithful will be alert, waiting, and not surprised. "So you also must be ready, because the Son of Man will come at an hour when you do not expect him" (Matthew 24:44).

When considering our Lord's prophetic parable of the virgins, would it be the wise or foolish virgins that the groom came upon and found unprepared? Would the groom come unexpectedly to those keeping watch and prepared, or to those who were not ready? Our Lord's words in this parable of the virgins are clear; no one knew when Rosh Hashanah would be fulfilled; however, He does not come as a thief to those who are prepared. "Afterward the other virgins came also, saying, 'Lord, lord, open to us.' But he answered, 'Truly, I say to you, I do not know you.' Watch therefore, for you know neither the day nor the hour" (Matthew 25:11–13, ESV). Our Lord made it clear in His revelation to John that if we do not wake up, He will come upon us as a thief, and then through our lack of preparation we will not know when He would come (Revelation 3:3).

Now let's take a look at another Scripture often quoted when discussing end-times fulfillment. "He said to them: 'It is not for you to know the times or dates the Father has set by his own authority'" (Acts 1:7).

What was Jesus responding to when He spoke these words? His disciples had come to Him and asked, "Lord, are You at this time going to restore the kingdom to Israel?" (Acts 1:6). The disciples asked if the kingdom was to be reestablished on earth at that time, and His response showed that this matter wasn't their concern. After all, was He not speaking to the men before Him when He said it did not belong to them to know the times and dates? It simply wasn't their responsibility to know when our Lord was to reestablish His kingdom on earth. Instead, it was their responsibility to recognize the times in which they lived, and the prophecies being fulfilled in their day, not events to occur long after their earthly lives.

Think about this: Our Lord criticized the elders of His day for not knowing the times and dates in which they lived. "Hypocrites! You know how to interpret the appearance of the earth and the sky. How is it that you don't know how to interpret this present time?" (Luke 12:56). Those men of authority should have been looking for the Mashiach during that specific time. Based on the seventy weeks prophecy alone, they had everything they needed to understand the exact day our Lord would appear. And then after that, the works our Lord accomplished would have been a glaring confirmation of His rightful lineage. So when they failed to understand the times and dates in which they lived, our Lord criticized them for not recognizing Him. "You know how to interpret the appearance of the sky, but you cannot interpret the signs of the times" (Matthew 16:3).

It was not the disciples' job to concern themselves with the times in which our Lord was to restore His kingdom to the earth; but instead, they were admonished to understand the times in which they lived. It is our responsibility to understand the times in which we live; so that when our Lord does return, He knocks and enters freely, instead of coming as a thief unbeknown to us to remove our names from the Book of Life.

In light of our Lord's own words, when someone says to us, "It does not belong to you to know the times and dates," we can express that it does belong to us to understand the times in which we live. Would we wish to find ourselves as the elders of Jesus's day, who were like the unwise virgins, not understanding the times in which they lived?

To believe that God would not have His prophets in the time of the end who understood how and when the Lord would return the kingdom of God to the earth is not biblically supported. God had always made it clear to His prophets beforehand the events that were about to unfold. From Noah to Moses and Jonah, God always sent His prophets to mankind to educate them before prophetic events were to occur. Through biblical precedent, we are assured that just as in the days of old, this will also be done in like manner during the time of the end.

> Indeed, the Sovereign LORD never does anything until he reveals his plans to his servants the prophets. (Amos 3:7, NLT)

And I will appoint my two witnesses, and they will prophesy for 1,260 days, clothed in sackcloth.
(Revelation 11:3)

Chapter 2:6

# The Temple Sanctuary

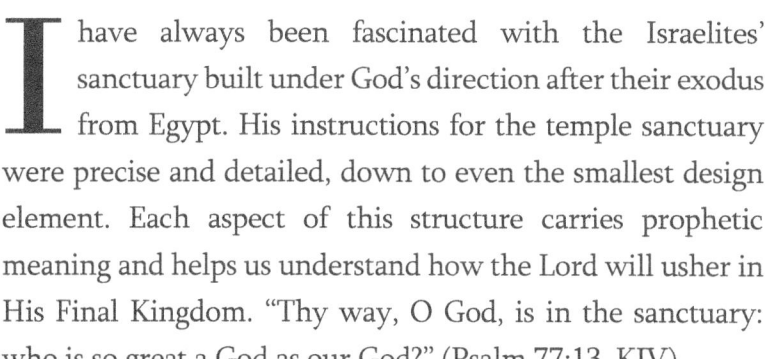

I have always been fascinated with the Israelites' sanctuary built under God's direction after their exodus from Egypt. His instructions for the temple sanctuary were precise and detailed, down to even the smallest design element. Each aspect of this structure carries prophetic meaning and helps us understand how the Lord will usher in His Final Kingdom. "Thy way, O God, is in the sanctuary: who is so great a God as our God?" (Psalm 77:13, KJV).

This tent-like structure was created to be mobile; after all, the Israelites spent forty years wandering the desert before entering the promised land. So its construction was made to be assembled and disassembled quite readily.

The tent was to be centrally located within the camp, having the twelve tribes stationed all around it in their places. While the priests had charge over the sanctuary's day-to-day activities, the people would bring in their sacrifices in order to have their sins forgiven.

When walking up to the structure itself, one would have been greeted by the 150-ft-wide by 75-ft-long white curtain surrounding the entire outer courtyard. These pure white curtains standing nearly seven and a half feet tall represented the righteousness of those who would enter the enclosure itself. "I answered, 'Sir, you know.' And he said, 'These are they who have come out of the great tribulation; they have washed their robes and made them white in the blood of the Lamb'" (Revelation 7:14). It is in the symbolism of these curtains that we are reminded of how we must be steadfast and resolved in our service of God's kingdom. "Enlarge the place of your tent, stretch your tent curtains wide, do not hold back; lengthen your cords, strengthen your stakes" (Isaiah 54:2).

As we made our way to the courtyard entrance, we would have been met by a gate measuring thirty feet wide and made up of brilliantly woven cloth of blue, purple, and scarlet. "For the entrance to the courtyard, provide a curtain twenty cubits long, of blue, purple, and scarlet yarn and finely twisted linen—the work of an embroiderer—with four posts and four bases" (Exodus 27:16). This gate represents none other than our Lord Christ Jesus Himself.

He is the gate and the way into God's organizational arrangement. "I am the gate; whoever enters through me will be saved. They will come in and go out, and find pasture" (John 10:9). The blue represented the loyalty of Christ, while the purple represented His royalty. The scarlet represents His blood, shed on behalf of those who would have their robes cleansed by it, through Him.

As one entered through the gate, you would find yourself within the outer courtyard of the sanctuary itself. This courtyard represents God's organizational arrangement on earth, made up of all those of mankind who wish to serve God's kingdom through Christ. "I was given a reed like a measuring rod and was told, 'Go and measure the temple of God and the altar, with its worshipers. But exclude the outer court; do not measure it, because it has been given to the Gentiles. They will trample on the holy city for 42 months'" (Revelation 11:1–2).

The first object to be seen within the outer walls would be the Brazen Altar. This altar would have been the location where the daily sacrifices were offered and was representative of the eventual sacrifice of our Lord Christ Jesus Himself.

The next object to be seen within the courtyard would have been the Bronze Laver, a water basin from which the priests would have cleansed themselves, representing the washing away of one's sins. Of interesting note: This water basin was made up of mirrors collected from the Israelite women. At that time, a highly polished piece of brass would have been the preferred material for a mirrored surface; their use in building the water basin shows how one must look within oneself when having sins washed away. We must understand and freely admit our sins for them to be washed away (Exodus 38:8).

Given that the sanctuary was always positioned pointing east, each object one gradually approached would have shone brilliantly in the warm glow of the rising sun. No different was the very gate of the tent itself. Again, one would find another door made of handwoven cloth of blue, purple, and scarlet, representative of our Lord; but this time, only the priests could enter through this door, after their cleansing from the laver (John 14:6).

Once the priests had entered the first room of the tent known as the Holy Place, they would have seen three different objects within. The table of showbread would have been just to their right and contained twelve loaves of bread, each representing one of the twelve tribes of Israel (Leviticus 24:8). Prophetic of things to come, these twelve loaves also represent the 144,000 co-rulers seen with Christ in the time of the end (Revelation 7:1–8).

To the priests' left stood the menorah, a candlestick made up of seven burners. This candlestick would have lighted the Holy Place for the priests and represented the Word of God that showed the way for their path. "Your word is a lamp for my feet, a light on my path" (Psalm 119:105).

Situated toward the back of the Holy Place stood the incense altar, while as incense was burned upon it, the smoke would rise to a hole in the top of the curtain separating the Holy Place from the next compartment beyond, the Most Holy Place. This incense represented the prayers of God's people entering heaven itself (Revelation 8:3–4). Again, another representation of our Lord Himself, this curtain was made up of intricately woven blue, purple, and scarlet thread representing the path by which the twelve loaves depictive of the 144,000 would enter the Holy Place of heaven. Paul spoke of this very matter after this curtain was ripped in two on the evening of our Lord's Sacrifice, representing the way into heaven being opened through His conquering the world. "Therefore, brothers and sisters, since we have confidence to enter the Most Holy Place by the blood of Jesus, by a new and living way opened for us through the curtain, that is, his body" (Hebrews 10:19–20).

When studying the tabernacle commissioned by God unto the Israelites, we are studying prophecy. Built within its structure is a prophetic map for us to understand end-time fulfillment. "They serve at a sanctuary that is a copy and shadow of what is in heaven. This is why Moses was warned when he was about to build the tabernacle: 'See to it that you make everything according to the pattern shown you on the mountain'" (Hebrews 8:5).

In the time of the end, the courtyard surrounding the spiritual temple, representing God's earthly organization, will be trampled on for 1,260 days. "But exclude the outer court; do not measure it, because it has been given to the Gentiles. They will trample on the holy city for forty-two months" (Revelation 11:2). The tent itself, representing the holy ones, is untouched, for the abomination is not placed within the prophetic Holy Place until the 1,290th day, thirty days after the courtyard is reestablished and our Lord is given rulership of the earthly kingdom.

How could one not be in awe of the astounding foresight and careful attention God has given us throughout His holy texts? He has prepared all things in their times, from the beginning to the end!

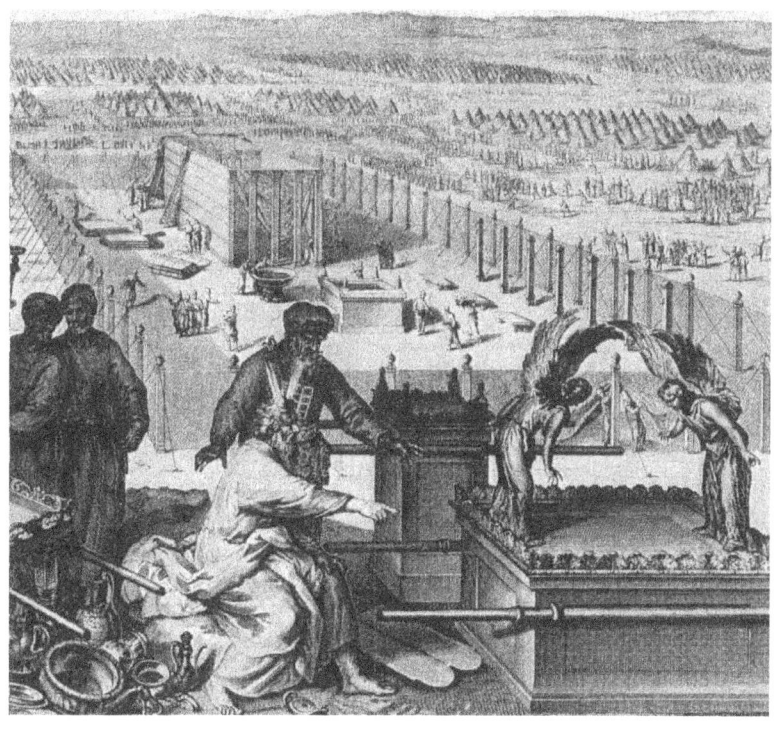

Blessed are those who wash their robes, that they may have the right to the tree of life and may go through the gates into the city. (Revelation 22:14)

Chapter 2:7

# Resurrection

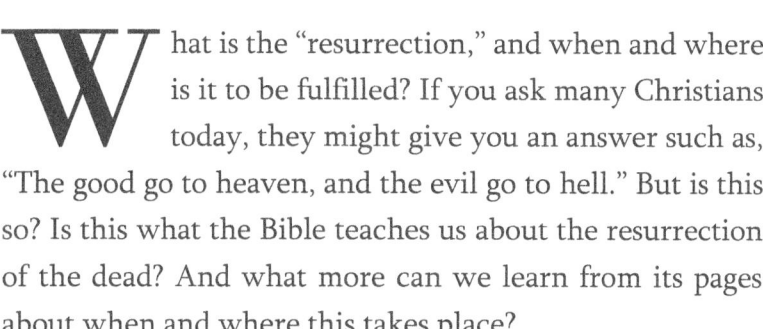

What is the "resurrection," and when and where is it to be fulfilled? If you ask many Christians today, they might give you an answer such as, "The good go to heaven, and the evil go to hell." But is this so? Is this what the Bible teaches us about the resurrection of the dead? And what more can we learn from its pages about when and where this takes place?

Simply put, there are three resurrections of the dead, and the study of their times and places will give us a better understanding of God's plans for His Final Kingdom.

There is a time period after Armageddon known as the thousand years of Christ's rule (Revelation 20:4). Newly resurrected ones from the past who never had the opportunity will learn of their Creator while either submitting to His rule or subsequently to their own selfish desires. "For he has set a day when he will judge the world with justice by the man he has appointed. He has given proof of this to everyone by raising him from the dead" (Acts 17:31).

During this time, many will be given the opportunity to go on to either eternal life or to everlasting shame. "Multitudes who sleep in the dust of the earth will awake: some to everlasting life, others to shame and everlasting contempt" (Daniel 12:2). You see, there have been countless individuals throughout human history who have never had the opportunity to learn of their Creator or to have shown themselves faithful toward God's rule, and it will be during these thousand years that they will be afforded the opportunity to do so.

When these prophecies of the resurrected in Daniel chapter 12 were written, they denoted the fate of these at the end of the thousand-year reign of Christ, when they will have either become righteous or wicked. Prophecy is often written in the past tense, for all things have already occurred with God. When resurrected into the rule of Christ, they will be neither righteous nor wicked, for that is determined by their future conduct. "And I have the same hope in God as these men themselves have, that there will be a resurrection of both the righteous and the wicked" (Acts 24:15).

There is another group of people to enter this thousand-year reign of Christ, and they will need no resurrection at all. These are those who survive Armageddon itself. "Then one of the elders asked me, 'These in white robes—who are they, and where did they come from?' I answered, 'Sir, you know.' And he said, 'These are they who have come out of the great tribulation; they have washed their robes and made them white in the blood of the Lamb'" (Revelation 7:13–14). Imagine that prospect, never having to die at all! Truly, what a wonderful outlook for those alive in the time of our Lord's arrival.

During this period, humanity will rule in the image of God, just as they were always intended to do, as they return the entire earth to a paradise state, which Adam and Eve had lost. For Satan himself will not be present and will be bound in chains, thrown into an abyss for a thousand years, away from any possibility of influencing our Lord's kingdom. "And I saw an angel coming down out of heaven, having the key to the Abyss and holding in his hand a great chain. He seized the dragon, that ancient serpent, who is the devil, or Satan, and bound him for a thousand years" (Revelation 20:1–2). Under the direction of Christ Jesus and His co-rulers, the earth will grow and prosper in abundant peace.

So then, we have identified one resurrection in the thousand-year reign of Christ; what about the other two groups?

The second group of people in our discussion of the resurrections are the co-rulers with Christ. On the night of His arrest, Christ Jesus established a new covenant for a kingdom with His disciples. These are said to be part of a first resurrection. "For the Lord himself will come down from heaven, with a loud command, with the voice of the archangel and with the trumpet call of God, and the dead in Christ will rise first" (1 Thessalonians 4:16).

> I saw thrones on which were seated those who had been given authority to judge. And I saw the souls of those who had been beheaded because of their testimony about Jesus and because of the word of God. They had not worshiped the beast or its image and had not received its mark on their foreheads or their hands. They came to life and reigned with Christ a thousand years. (Revelation 20:4)

Those who are resurrected under the new covenant arrangement to rule are part of the first resurrection. As mentioned in the chapter Time of the End, these are the ones dead in Christ, who will be resurrected on Yom Kippur when God's kingdom is established on earth, and their brothers yet still alive in the world are transfigured. "In a flash, in the twinkling of an eye, at the last trumpet. For the trumpet will sound, the dead will be raised imperishable, and we will be changed" (1 Corinthians 15:52). In the covenant arrangement with Christ, these are said not to be affected by the second death, for they will be transferred unto heaven. "This is the first resurrection. Blessed and holy are those who share in the first resurrection. The second death has no power over them, but they will be priests of God and of Christ and will reign with him for a thousand years" (Revelation 20:5–6).

This second death occurs at the end of the thousand-year rule of Christ, representing a final judgment from which there is no return. This will be the time when those living will have been declared either righteous or unrighteous after Satan is let loose for a period of time to influence the world once again. "When the thousand years are over, Satan will be released from his prison and will go out to deceive the nations in the four corners of the earth—Gog and Magog—and to gather them for battle" (Revelation 20:7–8). In accord with their deeds, all humanity will be righteous or unrighteous at the end of these one thousand years. Each will either be found written in the Book of Life or thrown into the lake of fire (Revelation 20:13–15).

Then we come to the third resurrection of our discussion. "The rest of the dead did not come to life until the thousand years were ended" (Revelation 20:5). Ending the thousand years of Christ's rule, and after Satan is thrown into the lake of fire, there is the third resurrection. At this point, everyone found written in the Book of Life is raised into the cleansed kingdom of God. "And I saw the dead, great and small, standing before the throne, and books were opened. Another book was opened, which is the Book of Life. The dead were judged according to what they had done as recorded in the books" (Revelation 20:12).

Those included in this third resurrection are all the faithful ones from the past. If we think about it rationally, individuals such as John the Baptist need not be resurrected into the thousand-year reign of Christ, for his faithfulness was already proven unto death. His name is already written in the Book of Life. Thus, he will be resurrected after Satan is destroyed at the end of the thousand-year reign.

It should be obvious as well that there will no doubt be billions of humans living on earth at the end of the thousand years when Satan is let loose again, and no doubt there will be countless who will fall away from God's way of rule at that time. "In number they are like the sand on the seashore" (Revelation 20:8). Therefore, once the earth is cleansed for a final time, countless faithful from the past will be resurrected into God's newly reestablished kingdom! "Blessed are the meek, for they will inherit the earth" (Matthew 5:5).

After the final resurrection of those whose names are written in the Book of Life, Hades, the common grave of mankind, will be done away with forever. Death will be no more, and God's kingdom will flourish into all eternity. "Then death and Hades were thrown into the lake of fire. The lake of fire is the second death" (Revelation 20:14). At this time, our Lord Christ Jesus will hand the restored kingdom back to His Father, so that He may be all, in all:

> Then the end will come, when he hands over the kingdom to God the Father after he has destroyed all dominion, authority, and power. For he must reign until he has put all his enemies under his feet. The last enemy to be destroyed is death. For he "has put everything under his feet." Now when it says that "everything" has been put under him, it is clear that this does not include God himself, who put everything under Christ. When he has done this, then the Son himself will be made subject to him who put everything under him, so that God may be all in all. (1 Corinthians 15:24–28)

Never will this subject of God's right to rule be challenged again, as those who serve on the side of righteousness go on to endure for all eternity!

These are the two who are anointed to serve the Lord of all the earth. (Zechariah 4:14)

# Part Three
# A Witness

Chapter 3:1

# The Israel of God

Who are God's people? In ancient times, a group of people known as the Hebrews were set aside for particular use by God for more than two millennia. Through their line of succession, a king would be born who would bring about the forgiveness of sin and facilitate the arrival of God's Final Kingdom on earth. Throughout history, scholars have debated several identities of modern-day Israel, and it is this subject which we are going to address here.

Beginning with Abraham of old, God promised a genetic line that would fulfill prophecy pertaining to His kingdom's establishment, a covenant promised through King David for an heir who would rule God's kingdom to come.

Which brings us to our first question: Were the Hebrews, or descendants of Abraham, the only people on earth who had the prospect of forgiveness of sin and, therefore, the hope of a resurrection? Indeed, this is not so, for God's love extends to all people. We know that people from other nations were under God's command as well; for whenever a member of another nation was to reside within the household of a Hebrew, they were expected to live as a Hebrew, undergoing circumcision in conjunction with the covenant arrangement by God (Exodus 12:44).

Therefore, a covenant arrangement is simply a matter of prophecy unto God's people to understand the appointed times, whether of our Lord's first arrival or His second. It can be said that the Jewish nation did not have a monopoly on God's love; however, His setting aside of the Jewish nation for prophetic use was to fulfill His promise announced in the Garden of Eden. "And I will put enmity between you and the woman, and between your offspring and hers; he will crush your head, and you will strike his heel" (Genesis 3:15). Many other nations existed alongside the ancient Hebrews, and, no doubt, countless from among those nations will be resurrected into God's kingdom (Romans 2:12–16).

The Bible concerns itself much with the identification of God's people, and this brings us to a critical identifier as to who represents the modern-day fulfillment of the Jewish nation in prophecy.

As was written in the chapter entitled Seventy Weeks, the Davidic covenant was fulfilled from our Lord's baptism to Cornelius's baptism. Ending the seventieth week marked the inclusion of people from all nations into the new covenant arrangement, in fulfillment of Peter's vision of the sheet descending from heaven (Acts 10:9–16). From that moment on, anyone being baptized in conjunction with that new covenant was to be known as a Jew. These are the ones who make up the Israelite nation of prophecy today. No more was a Jew a matter of race or location, but that of all believers under their common faith in our Lord Christ Jesus:

> A person is not a Jew who is one only outwardly, nor is circumcision merely outward and physical. No, a person is a Jew who is one inwardly; and circumcision is circumcision of the heart, by the Spirit, not by the written code. Such a person's praise is not from other people, but from God. (Romans 2:28–29)

> For there is no difference between Jew and Gentile— the same Lord is Lord of all and richly blesses all who call on Him, for, "Everyone who calls on the name of the Lord will be saved." (Romans 10:12–13)

As for prophetic fulfillment of prophecy, the outward identity of race is meaningless and has no place in the worship of God's kingdom in our day. Prophecy concerns itself with fulfillment, and metaphoric identifiers within the text merely assist the Lord's prophets in understanding appointed times. So then, after Cornelius was baptized into the new covenant arrangement, the nature of one being a Jew, within the text, amounted to all believing Christians. "Understand, then, that those who have faith are children of Abraham" (Galatians 3:7). As well, in like manner at this moment, Jerusalem and its constituent parts, including the Temple itself, all become metaphoric. The Temple of God is no longer a location or place; it is now within each of us under the new covenant of Christ. "Don't you know that you yourselves are God's temple and that God's Spirit dwells in your midst?" (1 Corinthians 3:16).

Now let us discuss more specifically the idea that a Jew in prophecy represents a descended genetic Jew in our day, as many believe. When studying family trees, for each generation one looks back, the number of descendants doubles. Using an average of a generation amounting to thirty years, if one counts their genealogy back to the year seventy of our common era, we discover that we would have twenty quintillion ancestors. That is a twenty with eighteen zeros behind it! Now there were not that many people alive in the first century. There were probably only around two hundred million living at that time. The discrepancy amounts to the many duplicate names on such a list as families overlapped throughout generations.

Now let us say the Jewish population of the first century amounted to approximately 5 percent of the world's population. That would mean that everyone living today has twenty quintillion opportunities to have been a descendant of one of Abraham's 5 percent lineage from the first century. After all, when Rome destroyed Jerusalem in 70 CE, the remaining Jewish descendants were spread throughout all mankind. If you had those percentage odds of winning a prize and bought twenty quintillion tickets for that prize, do you think you would have a chance to win? Therefore, there is no such thing as a physical bloodline within prophecy today; for no one can trace their lineage back throughout all ancient history. Being a Jew, according to the Apostle Paul, wasn't determined by the percentage of genetics one had in their blood; a Jew was one of the heart (Romans 2:29).

It is for this very reason God told us specifically not to be part of the controversies of endless genealogies:

> But avoid foolish controversies and genealogies and arguments and quarrels about the law, because these are unprofitable and useless. (Titus 3:9)

> As I urged you when I went into Macedonia, stay there in Ephesus so that you may command certain people not to teach false doctrines any longer or to devote themselves to myths and endless genealogies. Such things promote controversial speculations rather than advancing God's work—which is by faith. (1 Timothy 1:3–4)

> There is neither Jew nor Gentile, neither slave nor free, nor is there male and female, for you are all one in

> Christ Jesus. If you belong to Christ, then you are Abraham's seed, and heirs according to the promise. (Galatians 3:28–29)
>
> It is not as though God's word had failed. For not all who are descended from Israel are Israel. (Romans 9:6)
>
> Nor because they are his descendants are they all Abraham's children. On the contrary, "It is through Isaac that your offspring will be reckoned." In other words, it is not the children by physical descent who are God's children, but it is the children of the promise who are regarded as Abraham's offspring. (Romans 9:7–8)

This may come as a shock to many Christians in our modern world, but Israel, Jerusalem, and the Jewish nation in prophecy of the end times have nothing to do with a physical location in the Middle East, nor any racially ethnic people. The Israel of God is made up of all true believers in Christ, just as in the same way the prophesied Jerusalem to be surrounded and the Temple to be rebuilt are metaphors of all peoples within our Lord's spiritual arrangement on earth today. "Do you not know that you are God's temple and that God's Spirit dwells in you?" (1 Corinthians 3:16).

All you who read this and have faith are the Israel of God, the very ones spoken of as His people. "Neither circumcision nor uncircumcision means anything; what counts is the new creation. Peace and mercy to all who follow this rule—to the Israel of God" (Galatians 6:15–16).

When prophecy speaks of the future Jerusalem being surrounded and the courtyard trampled for forty-two months, it speaks of a metaphoric representation of God's spiritual organization on earth rather than any specific location on a map (Luke 21:20; Revelation 11:1–2). We will recognize God's modern organizational arrangement when their apostasy comes to light and their preaching work ceases in fulfillment of the timeline set out in Daniel's prophecy.

Chapter 3:2

# The Great Apostasy

Did you know that God's kingdom will not come unless an apostasy comes first? "Let no one in any way deceive you, for it will not come unless the apostasy comes first, and the man of lawlessness is revealed, the son of destruction" (2 Thessalonians 2:3, NASB). If we wish to identify the coming of God's kingdom, this seems a pretty significant point to consider. So let us start with a definition of that word *apostasy*.

> A-pos'-ta-si = (*apostasia*, "a standing away from"): i.e. a falling away, a withdrawal, a defection.

Used twice in the New Testament, *apostasia* expresses abandonment of the faith or rebellion on the part of God's people. According to 2 Thessalonians 2:3, God's kingdom will not come unless a rebellion on the part of His people becomes manifest to all. Does this sound familiar? In the chapter entitled Chronology, we read of a rebellion on the part of God's people that will ultimately result in the removal of the daily sacrifice. "Because of rebellion, the Lord's people and the daily sacrifice were given over to it" (Daniel 8:12). We also saw how today that daily sacrifice pertains to the preaching work of God's people to mankind. No doubt, this rebellion will serve as a catalyst to assist God's people in recognizing that their Lord is near the door and His hour of judgment is at hand. "For it is time for judgment to begin with God's household; and if it begins with us, what will the outcome be for those who do not obey the gospel of God?" (1 Peter 4:17).

Prophesied thousands of years ago, this falling away of God's people from true worship shows itself in multiple fulfillments throughout different times outlined in the Bible (Ecclesiastes 1:9). By these previous fulfillments, one can identify the modern-day representation of the daily sacrifice itself. If we are to discern our Lord's organizational arrangement on earth, we will need to recognize their apostasy when manifested on a worldwide stage. So let's break it out into its segmented parts to understand better what is to come.

In starting, we are told some of God's people will turn their ears away from the truth and begin to pay attention to false stories. "They will turn their ears away from the truth and turn aside to myths" (2 Timothy 4:4). These myths, or false stories, are teachings from demons that lure away God's people from true worship. "The Spirit clearly says that in later times some will abandon the faith and follow deceiving spirits and things taught by demons" (1 Timothy 4:1). What are these myths and deceiving spirits that bring about a rebellion on the part of God's people?

In the thirteenth chapter of Revelation, we read of a mark of the beast without which people are restricted from buying or selling. "It also forced all people, great and small, rich and poor, free and slave, to receive a mark on their right hands or on their foreheads, so that they could not buy or sell unless they had the mark, which is the name of the beast or the number of its name" (Revelation 13:16–17). We know the buying and selling in Revelation are not physical commerce of this world; for Christ Jesus our Lord told us Himself in this very same book that the buying and selling are spiritual matters and not an exchange of goods. "I counsel you to buy from me gold refined in the fire, so you can become rich; and white clothes to wear, so you can cover your shameful nakedness; and salve to put on your eyes, so you can see" (Revelation 3:18).

So to understand what spiritual matter this mark of the beast represents, let's take a closer look at that mark itself and what it represents. "This calls for wisdom. Let the person who has insight calculate the number of the beast, for it is the number of a man. That number is 666" (Revelation

13:18). It is pretty easy to identify what this number represents, as there are a few places in Scripture that discuss this very same mark, as seen in Revelation chapter 13.

To begin, that eighteenth verse identifies this 666 number as "a man's number." Who is this man? He represents the fall of anyone from true worship, just like that of King Solomon. "The weight of the gold that Solomon received yearly was 666 talents" (1 Kings 10:14). Later in life, Solomon began to fall away from true worship and rebel by taking more unto himself than God commanded; thus, his actions resulted in his apostasy (Deuteronomy 17:16–18). This 666 number represents a falling away from true worship and a rebellion against God's commands. We will recognize the apostasy to come through this mark, culminating in the daily sacrifice being removed when God's people are no longer allowed to preach of His kingdom to come.

In the book of Daniel, we have further confirmation of this 666 number and its representation of apostasy from God Himself. "King Nebuchadnezzar made an image of gold, sixty cubits high and six cubits wide, and set it up on the plain of Dura in the province of Babylon" (Daniel 3:1). King Nebuchadnezzar set up an image in Babylon that measured 60 x 6 x 6 cubits. Since we know this object to be three-dimensional, it most likely resembled an obelisk, such as is found in the Washington Monument in DC. Measuring a height of 555 feet tall and a width of 55 feet at its base, the

Washington Monument bears the same sort of comparative measurements as that which was set up in Babylon.

Now what is the narrative in Daniel chapter 3 when king Nebuchadnezzar commissions this structure to be built? He gives a command that everyone throughout his province must bow down and worship the image, or they shall die. "Whoever does not fall down and worship will immediately be thrown into a blazing furnace" (Daniel 3:6). Does this not sound exactly like the events laid out in Revelation chapter 13? The second beast of Revelation chapter 13 is also spoken of as causing fire to come down from heaven, facilitating the death of those who refuse to worship its image, represented by the number 666. These two prophecy examples stand as a glaring precedent on how Scripture uses itself to clarify the context.

Therefore, the number 666 represents the apostasy of God's people and that of being led away from true worship by the beast of Revelation chapter 13. He does this by establishing an agreement with those who have forsaken their position with God. "He will return and show favor to those who forsake the holy covenant" (Daniel 11:30). Those leaving the holy covenant will be doing so in agreement with the wild beast; in so doing, they will be seen taking the mark of apostasy from true worship. "With flattery he will corrupt those who have violated the covenant, but the people who know their God will firmly resist him" (Daniel 11:32).

At this point of corruption, true Christians will recognize prophecy's fulfillment through the apostasy of God's people, led by the so-called man of lawlessness. "Don't let anyone deceive you in any way, for that day will not come until the rebellion occurs and the man of lawlessness is revealed, the man doomed to destruction" (2 Thessalonians 2:3). This man of lawlessness appears to be the very same beast from Revelation and Daniel when they mention his exalting himself, deception, and placement within the temple of God. However, we should remember that while individual men run governmental agencies, these specific prophecies highlight the agencies themselves.

Through this corruption on the part of the man of lawlessness, the wild beast can accomplish its ultimate goal of coming against the preaching work by vigorously denouncing God's name and exposing those working contrary to God's will within His organizational arrangement on earth:

> The beast was given a mouth to utter proud words and blasphemies and to exercise its authority for forty-two months. It opened its mouth to blaspheme God, and to slander his name and his dwelling place and those who live in heaven. (Revelation 13:5–6)

> He will speak against the Most High and oppress his holy people and try to change the set times and the laws. The holy people will be delivered into his hands for a time, times and half a time. (Daniel 7:25)

What is the result of the apostasy on the part of God's people? The preaching work will cease, and His people will be brought into spiritual captivity for transgressions against the holy covenant. "Because of rebellion, the Lord's people and the daily sacrifice were given over to it. It prospered in everything it did, and truth was thrown to the ground" (Daniel 8:12). These will be the events upon which we will recognize the coming of God's kingdom.

It is apparent, however, that even before these appointed times, God's people will have built up sin for many years. Throughout the text, we are told that just as had befallen the Jewish nation of old, so befalls the leaders of God's people today. Those in charge of spiritual matters have treated the flock poorly, metaphorically flogging them and abandoning the sheep to their own devices.

> Son of man, prophesy against the shepherds of Israel; prophesy and say to them: "This is what the Sovereign Lord says: Woe to you shepherds of Israel who only take care of yourselves! Should not shepherds take care of the flock? You eat the curds, clothe yourselves with the wool, and slaughter the choice animals, but you do not take care of the flock. You have not strengthened the weak or healed the sick or bound up the injured. You have not brought back the strays or searched for the lost. You have ruled them harshly and brutally. So they were scattered because there was no shepherd, and when they were scattered they became food for all

the wild animals. My sheep wandered over all the mountains and on every high hill. They were scattered over the whole earth, and no one searched or looked for them." (Ezekiel 34:2–6)

So then, what precisely will we see first, to allow us to recognize the daily sacrifice when its removal sparks the arrival of the appointed times and the nearness of God's kingdom? Quite simply, we are told that those in charge of the flock of God profane His Holy Name in the sight of all mankind. "I will show the holiness of my great name, which has been profaned among the nations, the name you have profaned among them" (Ezekiel 36:23). Therefore, what we will see is God's name conveyed alongside wrongdoing on the part of those claiming to be spokesmen of God, fulfilling the appointed times and the judgment upon His own house. "For it is time for judgment to begin with God's household; and if it begins with us, what will the outcome be for those who do not obey the gospel of God?" (1 Peter 4:17).

No doubt, among these worldwide news events, it is possible that there shall even be individuals who have entered some agreement with the wild beast in the worship of its image. Perhaps the beast's mark will be some regulation set upon Christians to contradict or deny their pure worship, such as the command to young Daniel to eat from the table of the king of Babylon in contradiction to God's commands. Or perhaps some joint declaration of religions will be required among nations. *Whatever comes to transpire, it is evident that upon breaking world news in defamation of God's name, the countdown of our Lord's second coming and the arrival of His Final Kingdom will have begun!* Through these prophetic fulfillments, the man of lawlessness who will war against Christ will be revealed, just as the apostasy against God's name will be manifest among His people.

When we see all of these things start to occur, we should know and have faith; our Lord is close at hand! "Even so, when you see all these things, you know that it is near, right at the door" (Matthew 24:33). Remember, you and I are forewarned of these events and given foreknowledge of what is to come. Being aware of these things will help prevent us from becoming partakers in the fate of those acting against God's holy covenant. "Therefore, dear friends, since you have been forewarned, be on your guard so that you may not be carried away by the error of the lawless and fall from your secure position" (2 Peter 3:17).

Let us, therefore, pass through the fire, being refined spiritually rather than being numbered among those taking the mark of the beast. Just as Daniel's companions, who by fire faced death rather than worship an idol, let us be found worthy by not compromising our faith and yielding to apostasy!

> This third I will put into the fire; I will refine them like silver and test them like gold. They will call on my

name and I will answer them; I will say, "They are my people," and they will say, "The Lord is our God." (Zechariah 13:9)

I counsel you to buy from me gold refined in the fire, so you can become rich; and white clothes to wear, so you can cover your shameful nakedness; and salve to put on your eyes, so you can see. (Revelation 3:18)

Today, if you hear his voice, do not harden your hearts as you did in the rebellion. (Hebrews 3:15)

Chapter 3:3

# Two Witnesses

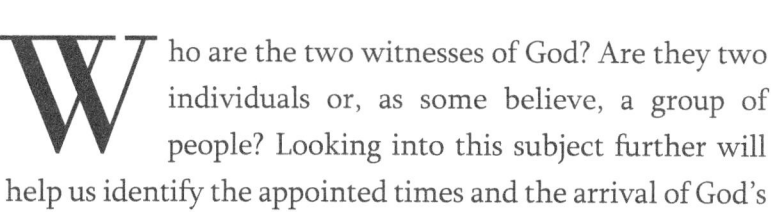

Who are the two witnesses of God? Are they two individuals or, as some believe, a group of people? Looking into this subject further will help us identify the appointed times and the arrival of God's Final Kingdom.

There are two places of considerable note in the Bible that discuss these two witnesses: the Revelation of Jesus Christ chapter 11 and Zechariah chapters 3 and 4.

The book of Revelation describes these two as prophets dressed in sackcloth, serving the Lord for 1,260 days. "And I will appoint my two witnesses, and they will prophesy for 1,260 days, clothed in sackcloth" (Revelation 11:3). As said previously, their wearing of sackcloth during this period represents their mourning the ceasing of the kingdom-preaching work (Revelation 11:2). It should be noted that this Scripture does not say forty-two months is the only time they serve as prophets, but that simply their wearing of sackcloth amounts to forty-two months.

In Revelation, these two are described as olive trees and lampstands. "They are 'the two olive trees' and the two lampstands, and 'they stand before the Lord of the earth'" (Revelation 11:4). The two witnesses of Revelation chapter 11 connect themselves directly to Zechariah chapter 4, where we read of them in similar terminology. "I see a solid gold lampstand with a bowl at the top and seven lamps on it, with seven channels to the lamps. Also, there are two olive trees by it, one on the right of the bowl and the other on its left" (Zechariah 4:2).

As one continues reading Zechariah chapter 4, in no uncertain terms, the text spells out exactly who these two olive trees represent, the two anointed ones:

> Then I said to him, "What are these two olive trees on the right and the left of the lampstand?" And a second time I answered and said to him, "What are these two branches of the olive trees, which are beside the two golden pipes from which the golden oil is poured out?" He said to me, "Do you not know what these are?" I said, "No, my lord." Then he said, "These are the two anointed ones who stand by the Lord of the whole earth." (Zechariah 4:11–14, ESV)

Now then, the question remains: Who do these two represent, individuals or a group of people? Let us start specifically with the statement in Zechariah 4:14 that reads, "These are the two anointed ones who stand by the Lord of the whole earth" (ESV).

Let's take a look at the exact context of this Scripture.

> These / Ãl-leh = These
>
> Two / Å¡e-nÃ = Two
>
> Ones / b̲e-nÃ- = Sons
>
> Anointed / hay-yiṣ-hār; = Oil

In this verse, "These" defines the group of whom we speak, the two previously mentioned olive trees.

"Two," as a noun, represents the number in this group. The group was already mentioned in the word "these."

"Ones," as a noun, denotes their position as sons of God.

"Anointed" defines their responsibility and position as they pertain to God's organizational arrangement.

Quite literally, this Scripture in Zechariah chapter 4 tells us that these two olive trees are two individuals. These "two ones" show their singleness without the need for interpolation (an insertion or addition). Therefore, it can be surmised that there shall be two individuals, just as Moses and Aaron who went to Pharaoh, who will represent the interests of God during the appointed times of the end.

If we notice back in Revelation chapter 11, these two anointed ones lay dead in the streets for three and a half days after being killed by the wild beast. These days cannot be anything other than three and a half literal days; for they cannot be connected to any other chronological time period within Scripture. If we endeavor to maintain uniform biblical precedence, just as the 1,260 days are simply that, so are the three and a half days just as they say.

During these forty-two months of mourning, the two witnesses' preaching work represents the time period after the daily sacrifice is removed until the Lord's rule is established on earth once again (Daniel 12:5–13). Ending the sixty-ninth week of Daniel chapter 9 completes these forty-two months, when their Lord is crowned over the earthly kingdom, restoring the spiritual courtyard, beginning the seventieth week, when Holy Spirit is poured out on all of God's people (Joel 2:28). At the halfway mark of this week, the two witnesses are killed, mirroring their Lord's example, in fulfillment of the first seventieth week, when He was sacrificed on behalf of humanity's sin.

In completion of that seventieth week, the two witnesses are resurrected in the sight of all mankind. *At that moment, an angel announces the coming kingdom of God unto all the world!* (Revelation 11:7–11, 14:6–7).

These two witnesses are named for us in the books of Zechariah chapters 3 and 4, as Joshua and Zerubbabel. While not these two literal men from the past, the two prophets in the time of the end will be two individuals of their day; for God has always used faithful men of their day to accomplish His will.

Each of the two is depicted as having their own responsibilities before the Lord. Joshua is given a stone with seven eyes, engraved by the Lord Himself. Zerubbabel is responsible for leveling out the land of God's holy mountain, representing the rebuilding work of God's spiritual temple on earth:

> "See, the stone I have set in front of Joshua! There are seven eyes on that one stone, and I will engrave an inscription on it," says the Lord Almighty, "and I will remove the sin of this land in a single day. (Zechariah 3:9)
>
> This is the word of the Lord to Zerubbabel: "Not by might nor by power, but by my Spirit," says the Lord Almighty. "What are you, mighty mountain? Before Zerubbabel you will become level ground. Then he will bring out the capstone to shouts of 'God bless it! God bless it!'" (Zechariah 4:6–7)

Many have believed Joshua of chapter 3 represents the Lord Jesus Himself; however, that simply is not so. To begin with, Joshua is seen wearing filthy garments, which are a sign of sin. "Now Joshua was dressed in filthy clothes as he stood before the angel" (Zechariah 3:3). This is not a matter of Jesus bearing our sins upon Himself, for the narrative shows that Joshua is given forgiveness from sin and reestablished from a previously unclean condition. In contrast, Scripture always depicts Jesus as sinless, the pure lamb, without blemish. The imagery of Zechariah chapter 3 even goes further in telling us that the Lord declares unto Joshua that "if" he walks in obedience with Him, he will be given "a" place among the angels of heaven (Zechariah 3:7). This is in striking contrast to the Lord Himself, who had already previously come from heaven (John 6:42). Quite simply, after Jesus had borne our sins through His sacrifice, there would have been no reason to address Him once again with words of "if" He would do God's will; at that point, He had died sinless.

There is, however, absolute proof to show that there is no way that Joshua can represent Jesus Himself. The Lord speaks to Joshua in the eighth verse, declaring that, in fact, Jesus is a separate personage from Joshua. "Listen, High Priest Joshua, you and your associates seated before you, who are men symbolic of things to come: I am going to bring my servant, the Branch" (Zechariah 3:8). Here, the branch spoken of is that of the line of David. In fulfillment of the Davidic covenant itself, our Lord's baptism was the fulfillment of David's lineage to rule over God's kingdom. "In those days and at that time I will make a righteous Branch sprout from David's line; he will do what is just and right in the land" (Jeremiah 33:15). Therefore, Joshua and Jesus are spoken of as two separate individuals in the third chapter of Zechariah.

We also have confirmation that the two witnesses are singular individuals of their time in our Lord's words about John the Baptist when He described him as the Elijah to come. As a type of Elijah, He showed that John did not need to be the literal reincarnation of that ancient patron to fulfill a prophetic role similar to the Elijah of old. While some believe these two will be literal resurrections of patriarchs from the past, scriptural precedence shows that these two individuals will be faithful men in their day:

> And the disciples asked him, "Then why do the scribes say that first Elijah must come?" He answered, "Elijah does come, and he will restore all things. But I tell you that Elijah has already come, and they did not recognize him but did to him whatever they pleased. So also the Son of Man will certainly suffer at their hands." Then the disciples understood that he was speaking to them of John the Baptist. (Matthew 17:10–13)

Now given we can comfortably surmise that these prophets represent two faithful individuals, let us take a closer look at their work and responsibilities.

It is apparent in Revelation that their work of prophecy is similar to that which Moses and Aaron delivered to Pharaoh of Egypt. Those two served as messengers of God's judgments upon that nation in order to bring His people out into a nation of their own. The two witnesses share a similar work as that of these two to Egypt, as further evidenced in their powers in the time of the end. "They have power to shut up the heavens so that it will not rain during the time they are prophesying; and they have power to turn the waters into blood and to strike the earth with every kind of plague as often as they want" (Revelation 11:6).

Just like those plagues announced to Egypt, the two witnesses in like manner will declare the Lord's judgments to the modern world, as recorded in the trumpets and bowls in Revelation. Look at the similarities between the plagues of Egypt and the plagues of Revelation:

> The first angel sounded his trumpet, and there came hail and fire mixed with blood, and it was hurled down on the earth. (Revelation 8:7)

> Then Moses stretched out his staff toward heaven, and the LORD sent thunder and hail, and fire ran down to the earth. And the LORD rained hail upon the land of Egypt. (Exodus 9:23, ESV)

> Then God's temple in heaven was opened, and within his temple was seen the ark of his covenant. And there came flashes of lightning, rumblings, peals of thunder, an earthquake and a severe hailstorm. (Revelation 11:19)

This is what the Lord says: By this you will know that I am the Lord: With the staff that is in my hand I will strike the water of the Nile, and it will be changed into blood. The fish in the Nile will die, and the river will stink; the Egyptians will not be able to drink its water. (Exodus 7:17–18)

The third angel poured out his bowl on the rivers and springs of water, and they became blood. (Revelation 16:4)

Then the Lord said to Moses, "Stretch out your hand toward the sky so that darkness spreads over Egypt—darkness that can be felt." (Exodus 10:21)

The fifth angel poured out his bowl on the throne of the beast, and its kingdom was plunged into darkness. (Revelation 16:10)

It will become fine dust over the whole land of Egypt, and festering boils will break out on people and animals throughout the land. (Exodus 9:9)

The first angel went and poured out his bowl on the land, and ugly, festering sores broke out on the people who had the mark of the beast and worshiped its image. (Revelation 16:2)

If you refuse to let them go, I will bring locusts into your country tomorrow. (Exodus 10:4)

And out of the smoke locusts came down on the earth and were given power like that of scorpions of the earth. (Revelation 9:3)

We see a direct correlation between the two witnesses' work in the appointed times and Moses and Aaron's work in Egypt. In like manner as these two prophets of old, the two witnesses' powers will lie in their message of God's judgments to the whole world. Rather than any physical fire protruding from their mouths, it is their fiery declarations of God's will that bring foreknowledge of the coming judgments on mankind.

Past patriarchs of the Bible serve as exemplars of how these two prophets of the end will accomplish God's work in a similar fashion. Just as seen in the transfiguration of Jesus on the mountain, Moses and Elijah stand alongside the Lord of the whole earth, in metaphoric symbolism of the two men to come, when in their time, they will accomplish similar prophetic works as those two faithful men from the past.

We read from the prophet Malachi about an Elijah to come before the day of the Lord. "See, I will send the prophet Elijah to you before that great and dreadful day of the Lord comes" (Malachi 4:5). From the ninth century BCE, the prophet Elijah was known for bringing God's judgments to the people of his day, in warning of the coming condemnation from God for their idolatrous ways. And by his example, we can surmise that the metaphoric Elijah to come will serve in just such a fashion.

As we know, John the Baptist served in a similar capacity as the prophet Elijah of old. However, was John's work in fulfillment of Malachi's prophecy of the Elijah to come before the day of the Lord? Though John served to a similar extent as Elijah, there is still yet another prophetic example of Elijah's coming. John himself even knew this when he exclaimed, "They asked him, 'Then who are you? Are you Elijah?' He said, 'I am not.' 'Are you the Prophet?' He answered, 'No'" (John 1:21). John wasn't contradicting our Lord by saying he didn't fulfill a role similar to the role of that prophet of old; he was simply answering as to that Elijah to come, before the day of the Lord. Therefore, John's answer to his not being that Elijah to come tells us that there is still yet another fulfillment of this prophetic type of God's servant.

Here are a few examples of Elijah's actions in the ninth century BCE and their connections to the two prophets' work at the time of the end:

Elijah stopped the rain for 1,260 days: "I assure you that there were many widows in Israel in Elijah's time, when the sky was shut for three and a half years and there was a severe famine throughout the land" (Luke 4:25).

Two witnesses stopped the rain for 1,260 days: "They have power to shut up the heavens so that it will not rain during the time they are prophesying" (Revelation 11:6).

Elijah caused fire to come down before his enemies: "Then the fire of the Lord fell and burned up the sacrifice, the wood, the stones and the soil, and also licked up the water in the trench" (1 Kings 18:38).

Two witnesses caused fire to kill their enemies: "If anyone tries to harm them, fire comes from their mouths and devours their enemies" (Revelation 11:5).

While it is evident that these two men during the appointed times are said to have powers similar to those of past patriarchs, it should not be assumed that the two witnesses would need to resort to physical manifestations of power. Revelation is given as a series of signs to show what is to come. Therefore, the powers indicated by these two are evidenced within the prophecies of the trumpets and bowls themselves and represent the foreknowledge of future prophetic events these two will declare.

The two witnesses in the time of the end will be identifiable by fulfillment of prophecies in accord with their commissions from God. It behooves us all to stay awake, keeping on the watch for our Lord's prophets, as we see that day drawing near (2 Timothy 4:5).

"What are you, mighty mountain? Before Zerubbabel you will become level ground. Then he will bring out the capstone to shouts of 'God bless it! God bless it!'" (Zechariah 4:7)

Chapter 3:4

# 7 Eyes, 7 Spirits, 7 Lamps

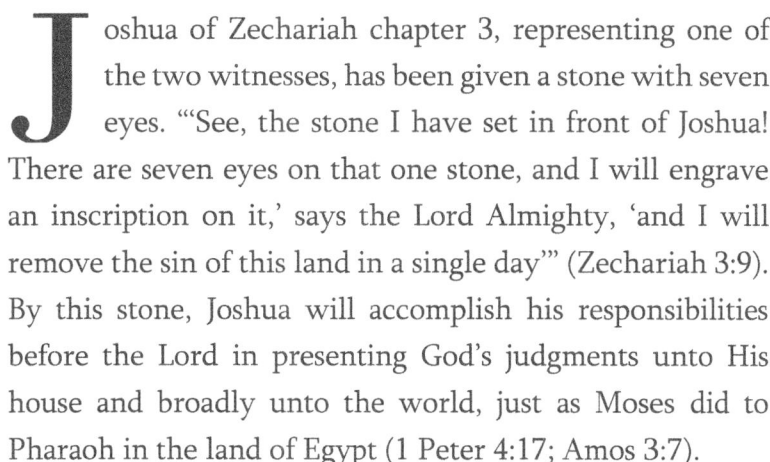

Joshua of Zechariah chapter 3, representing one of the two witnesses, has been given a stone with seven eyes. "'See, the stone I have set in front of Joshua! There are seven eyes on that one stone, and I will engrave an inscription on it,' says the Lord Almighty, 'and I will remove the sin of this land in a single day'" (Zechariah 3:9). By this stone, Joshua will accomplish his responsibilities before the Lord in presenting God's judgments unto His house and broadly unto the world, just as Moses did to Pharaoh in the land of Egypt (1 Peter 4:17; Amos 3:7).

The Hebrew word used here as a stone is the word *hā·'e·ḇen*. This is the same word used for the stone given to Moses containing the Ten Commandments. It is of significance that

Joshua would be seen with a stone similar to that which God had given Moses; for Joshua in the time of the end plays a similar prophetic role to that of Moses in Egypt.

There is yet another individual in the Bible described with a similar stone as is given Joshua, and that is the Joshua who came against Jericho during the sixteenth century before our common era. This servant of the Lord, for whom the book of Joshua is named, set up a stone before the people in remembrance of God's words to them. "And Joshua recorded these things in the Book of the Law of God. Then he took a large stone and set it up there under the oak near the holy place of the LORD" (Joshua 24:26). This stone would come to serve as a witness of the truth of God's commands, in justification of any future judgments by Him. "See!" he said to all the people. "This stone will be a witness against us. It has heard all the words the Lord has said to us. It will be a witness against you if you are untrue to your God" (Joshua 24:27).

Both the stones before Moses and the Joshua of old stood as reminders of God's Word, lest the people fall into apostasy, coming under judgment by Him (Joshua 24:23). Just as these two men are described with a stone representing God's Word, so does the Joshua to come. In his description, Joshua is given a stone inscribed by the Almighty Himself, and it is portrayed alongside the removal of sin on a single day. "'See, the stone I have set in front of Joshua! There are seven eyes on that one stone, and I will engrave an inscription on it,' says the LORD Almighty, 'and I will remove the sin of this land in a single day'" (Zechariah 3:9).

We know from our study of Zechariah that Joshua, from the building of the Second Temple period, represents a type of prophet that will be fulfilled in one of God's two witnesses. So then, this stone before him deserves a closer examination, as it pertains to our interest in the work of these two during the appointed times of the end.

Of significance pertaining to this stone before Joshua is the description of it containing seven eyes. "There are seven eyes on that one stone" (Zechariah 3:9). We have a descriptive explanation for these eyes in the next chapter of Zechariah, when we are told that Joshua's companion Zerubbabel is seen holding this very same stone. "Who are you, O great mountain? Before Zerubbabel you shall become a plain. And he shall bring forward the top stone amid shouts of 'Grace, grace to it!'" (Zechariah 4:7, ESV). The word used here as "stone" is that very same Hebrew word *hā·'e·ḇen* used in Zechariah chapter 3 and the stone seen held by Joshua. We have confirmation of this since verse 10 discusses the seven eyes that are upon it. "Who dares despise the day of small things, since the seven eyes of the Lord that range throughout the earth will rejoice when they see the chosen capstone in the hand of Zerubbabel?" (Zechariah 4:10). Therefore, we can say with certainty that the seven eyes upon the stone in front of Joshua represent the seven eyes of the Lord, ranging throughout all the earth.

It should be noted that many have taught that this stone before Joshua represents our Lord Christ Jesus Himself; however, this is also in error. Our Lord is always described as the cornerstone of God's organizational arrangement and not the top stone. "From Judah will come the cornerstone, from him the tent peg, from him the battle bow, from him every ruler" (Zechariah 10:4). In any building, the cornerstone sits at the bottom and represents the foundation stone that holds up the entire structure, without which the building would not stand. However, the capstone sits on the top of the structure, such as on a pyramid, and represents the culmination of said work. In no way does this stone represent any building's structural significance but rather that of a final puzzle piece on top.

As a plumbline before Zerubbabel, this capstone is said to assist him in rebuilding the spiritual temple and organizational arrangement by God on earth. Not unlike the stones before Moses and Joshua of old, the Word of God helps this prophet in returning true worship to His people under a singular faith in the time of the end.

Understanding that the eyes upon the stone before Joshua represent the eyes of the Lord, this guides us to the final book of the Bible, Revelation. "Then I saw a Lamb, looking as if it had been slain, standing at the center of the throne, encircled by the four living creatures and the elders. The Lamb had seven horns, and seven eyes, which are the seven spirits of God sent out into all the earth" (Revelation 5:6).

We are told here that these seven eyes represent the seven spirits of God, sent out into all the earth. This is a remarkably similar description to our stone in Zechariah, as the stone's eyes are said to range throughout all the world. Recognition that the stone before Joshua is representative of God's seven spirits will help us further our study of Joshua's role in God's kingdom during the appointed time.

There is another place in the book of Revelation that helps us highlight this prophecy relating to God's seven spirits, and that is chapter 4. "From the throne came flashes of lightning, rumblings and peals of thunder. In front of the throne, seven lamps were blazing. These are the seven spirits of God" (Revelation 4:5). Here we read of the seven spirits of God representing the seven lamps before His throne. What an incredible treasure hunt our Lord has provided for us within His Word. A trove of knowledge to assist those with interest in Scripture more than just at face value; for as we dive in deeper, we are rewarded with furthering our understanding of God's Word.

Before God's throne, these seven lamps should remind us of our study in the chapter entitled The Temple Sanctuary, where we discussed how the sanctuary established by the command of God represented heavenly matters (Hebrews 8:5). Within the Holy Place stood the menorah with seven lamps that lighted the way for the priest's steps. As a metaphoric depiction of God's Word, this lampstand typifies the very words of God by which the priests would live. "Your word is a lamp for my feet, a light on my path" (Psalm 119:105). Just as the menorah represented God's Word unto the priests of ancient Israel, so that lamp today is representative of the Bible itself that shines before the twelve loaves, prophetic of the 144,000 of God's faithful servants in the time of the end. "Then make its seven lamps and set them up on it so that they light the space in front of it" (Exodus 25:37).

By identifying the seven spirits of God representing the seven lamps in the Holy Place's modern-day fulfillment, one may confidently say that the capstone before Joshua is the final iteration of all prophetic law and prophecy to come. His responsibilities are in accord with bringing God's final judgments, not only to His own people but to those of the whole world. By this stone, the two witnesses, in the end, will be recognized as the prophetic events come to fruition.

As we have read, the Lord has given us a virtual trail to follow in understanding the textual context of this stone before Joshua. Just as through the depiction of these seven eyes as the seven spirits, representing those seven lamps before the throne of God, we are directed even further to a remarkably similar description when depicting God's throne in the book of Ezekiel. "The appearance of the living creatures was like burning coals of fire or like torches. Fire moved back and forth among the creatures; it was bright, and lightning flashed out of it" (Ezekiel 1:13). These torches or lamps visible here in this summarization of God's throne

## 7 Eyes, 7 Spirits, 7 Lamps

are just as described in the book of Revelation (Revelation 4:5). Of particular note, these torches before the throne burning with coals of fire will again help us further our understanding of the role that the Joshua to come plays in his work before the Lord.

In Ezekiel chapters 9 and 10, we see described a man dressed in linen. This depiction indicates this man's cleansed state from sin, not unlike that of Joshua in the third chapter of Zechariah when he is dressed in fine linen in conjunction with the forgiveness of sin (Ezekiel 9:1–2; Zechariah 3:3–4). In the vision contained in Ezekiel chapter 10, we are told this man dressed in linen reaches out into the burning coals from the very throne of God, where "torches" or "lamps" are described; and then, grabbing some of the fire, he tosses it over the city of God. "The Lord said to the man clothed in linen, 'Go in among the wheels beneath the cherubim. Fill your hands with burning coals from among the cherubim and scatter them over the city.' And as I watched, he went in" (Ezekiel 10:2).

Just as Joshua is given the capstone of the Word, this man in linen can be none other than that prophetic Joshua to come, one of the two witnesses. The fire from the very throne of God, representative of the judgments by Him, is cast over the city in accord with their sin and representative of the content of that stone itself (1 Peter 4:17). From the seven eyes of the stone to the seven eyes of the Lord, the seven spirits of God represent the seven lamps before the throne and the fiery judgments in accord with apostasy on the part of God's people. During the appointed times of the end, the two witnesses carry out their responsibilities before the Lord, just as Moses, Aaron, and Elijah had, in declaring those judgments before all mankind. Just as the example of Jericho's walls Joshua brings down through the seven trumpets, so the two witnesses bring forth the stone with seven eyes, in correspondence with the coming judgments of God.

It will be by fulfillment of their commissions that these two prophets are recognized. This stone before Joshua and Zerubbabel is the very capstone of the Word and ushers in the coming of His Final Kingdom.

So then, let us become one of those mentioned in Zechariah chapter 3 when it says of them, "Listen, High Priest Joshua, you and your associates seated before you, who are men symbolic of things to come" (Zechariah 3:8). Those who are said to be "symbolic" serve as portents or witnesses of the stone's fulfillment presented by the two witnesses. And in this way, you as a reader have the wonderful prospect of being part of this very prophecy when you see these events come to their completion, as laid out within the chronology of the Capstone.

# The Capstone

666: December 28, 2028 - Asara B'Tevet

•

Apostasy: September 10, 2029 - Rosh Hashanah

•

Walls Breached: July 6, 2033 - 9th Tammuz

•

Temple Destroyed: Aug 5, 2033 – 10th AV

•

State Collapse: Sep 27-Oct 4, 2034 - Sukkot

•

Coronation: October. 13, 2035 – Yom Kippur

•

The Final Kingdom: December 28, 2035 - Hanukkah

Chapter 3:5

# The Cup of Christ

One of the most cringe-worthy statements I hear many preachers of the Word today declare is that on the night of His arrest, our Lord doubted, or that while He prayed incessantly in the Garden of Gethsemane, He desired to get out of what was about to come upon Him. There could be nothing further from the truth, as this is simply a misunderstanding of the text that leads someone to such a conclusion. So with fresh eyes, let us look at the context of that night a little closer.

On the night of our Lord's arrest, He prayed vigorously to His Father that if it be His will, this cup would be removed from Him. "Father, if you are willing, take this cup from me; yet not my will, but yours be done" (Luke 22:42). Many have believed that our Lord's intention here was the desire that He not experience the events that He knew were about to occur. He already knew what was to come upon Him, as He had declared as much to His disciples just a few days before this. "We are going up to Jerusalem, and the Son of Man will be delivered over to the chief priests and the teachers of the law. They will condemn him to death and will hand him over to the Gentiles to be mocked and flogged and crucified. On the third day he will be raised to life!" (Matthew 20:18).

So then, He knew ahead of time, before He and His disciples even traveled to Jerusalem to celebrate the Passover festival, what awaited them there. But does this mean that Jesus was displaying doubt or misgivings about what He was about to experience? Not even in the slightest! In fact, not only was our Lord not showing any doubt or misgivings in His prayers, but He also expressed quite the opposite in His declarations by asking His Father to allow Him to continue to accomplish His purpose for coming to the earth in the first place!

You see, the cup our Lord asked His Father to remove did not represent the events that were about to come upon Him but instead represented that cup He offered His disciples that very night. As He and His disciples celebrated their final Passover festival together, our Lord took a cup, and after giving thanks, passed it to them.

> Then he took a cup, and when he had given thanks, he gave it to them, saying, 'Drink from it, all of you. This is my blood of the covenant, which is poured out for many for the forgiveness of sins.' (Matthew 26:27–28)

> "This cup is the new covenant between God and his people—an agreement confirmed with my blood." (1 Corinthians 11:25, NLT)

It was the cup representing the new covenant, and the bread representing His body (1 Corinthians 11:23–24).

So then, when on the night of our Lord's prayers in the Garden of Gethsemane, it was that cup He prayed His Father would remove from Him, meaning His life force on behalf of mankind. "Because the life of every creature is its blood" (Leviticus 17:14). He was, in all actuality, praying that He would fulfill what He came to earth to do. Far from doubting or wishing for the events prophesied not to come upon Him, He was so greatly anguished that He sweated blood, in evidence of just how earnest He was to fulfill His Father's will!

As an example of just how much our Lord abhorred any thought of not accomplishing His Father's will, we need only look to a conversation that I am sure Peter would have liked to have had back:

> From that time on Jesus began to explain to his disciples that he must go to Jerusalem and suffer many things at

the hands of the elders, the chief priests and the teachers of the law, and that he must be killed and on the third day be raised to life. Peter took him aside and began to rebuke him. "Never, Lord!" he said. "This shall never happen to you!" Jesus turned and said to Peter, "Get behind me, Satan! You are a stumbling block to me; you do not have in mind the concerns of God, but merely human concerns." (Matthew 16:21–23)

Jesus here chastised Peter for focusing on his human concerns, rather than keeping in mind God's thoughts. Our Lord was focused on accomplishing His Father's will rather than on any short-term personal gain. Jesus never once strayed from His responsibilities or His work before His Father. "The one who sent me is with me; he has not left me alone, for I always do what pleases him" (John 8:29). In no way would our Lord desire to circumvent His Father's will on the very night He was about to fulfill all He was sent to earth to do.

I have also heard these same misconceptions about our Lord's words just before He died. "About three in the afternoon Jesus cried out in a loud voice, 'Eli, Eli, lama sabachthani?' (which means 'My God, my God, why have you forsaken me?')" (Matthew 27:46). Many have said that our Lord doubted or felt His Father had abandoned Him because of the words He chose when just about to die. However, this is far from the truth. What our Lord was doing in the moments just before death was quoting

Scripture. In the song of David recorded for us in Psalms chapter 22, we find our Lord's words just before He died: "My God, my God, why have you forsaken me?" (Psalm 22:1). In contrast to any notion that He was contradicting His Father, our Lord here was quoting this very chapter to identify prophecies fulfilled in Him that very same day. In His final hour, His concerns were still for you and me:

> All who see me mock me; they hurl insults, shaking their heads. "He trusts in the Lord," they say, "let the Lord rescue him. Let him deliver him, since he delights in him." (Psalm 22:7–8)

> Now leave him alone. Let's see if Elijah comes to save him. (Matthew 27:49)

> My mouth is dried up like a potsherd, and my tongue sticks to the roof of my mouth; you lay me in the dust of death. (Psalm 22:15)

> Later, knowing that everything had now been finished, and so that Scripture would be fulfilled, Jesus said, "I am thirsty." (John 19:28)

> Dogs surround me, a pack of villains encircles me; they pierce my hands and my feet. (Psalm 22:16)

> This man was handed over to you by God's deliberate plan and foreknowledge; and you, with the help of wicked men, put him to death by nailing him to the cross. (Acts 2:23)

> They divide my clothes among them and cast lots for my garment. (Psalm 22:18)

> When they had crucified him, they divided up his clothes by casting lots. (Matthew 27:35)

Our Lord's recitation from the beautiful expressions of the psalmist highlights the plight of humanity and the accomplishment of establishing the way unto God! In our Lord's final moments, He was concentrating yet again on His Father's will, in accomplishing all He came here to do. By His selfless actions, all mankind has the prospect of everlasting life through Him.

> From you comes the theme of my praise in the great assembly; before those who fear you I will fulfill my vows. The poor will eat and be satisfied; those who seek the Lord will praise him—may your hearts live forever! All the ends of the earth will remember and turn to the Lord, and all the families of the nations will bow down before him, for dominion belongs to the Lord and he rules over the nations. All the rich of the earth will feast and worship; all who go down to the dust will kneel before him—those who cannot keep themselves alive. Posterity will serve him; future generations will be told about the Lord. They will proclaim his righteousness, declaring to a people yet unborn: He has done it! (Psalm 22:25–31)

He has indeed done it! He has fulfilled all His Father sent Him to do. In so doing, He has become the gateway to all mankind who exercise faith in Him. Through Him is eternal life, and infinite blessings from God the Father, throughout all eternity!

The next time you hear our Lord's words just before His death, "My God, My God, why have You forsaken Me?" remember the purpose of those words: that all He had come to accomplish, "He has done it!" (Psalm 22:31).

Chapter 3:6

# The Correct Bible Translation

There seems to be an endless debate about which translation of the Holy Scriptures is most accurate and appropriate for biblical studies. We also hear the arguments that some translations should be shunned or avoided as being against the will of God Himself, for one reason or the other. So what should be understood as the correct Bible translation, and which one should we be using?

The answer to that is: It depends. The correct translation of the Bible one should be using depends on their level of understanding within the text itself. You see, if someone requires the milk of Scripture, the answer to the right translation for them is: Any Bible is correct! "Brothers and sisters, I could not address you as people who live by the Spirit but as people who are still worldly—mere infants in Christ. I gave you milk, not solid food, for you were not yet ready for it. Indeed, you are still not ready" (1 Corinthians 3:1–2). Any Bible is a useful tool in the hands of someone new to the text, simply in getting them started reading.

To get new ones caught up in the debate about accurate translations is to introduce unnecessary burden and prejudice to a young faith. Just because you feel as though it is of the utmost importance for a new believer to use a particular translation, that does not mean this is the best topic to focus on with them. Any of the numerous translations available can serve a young one in scriptural study adequately when just starting out learning of the true God.

It is my opinion that there are many pastors and parishioners alike who would be very well served by reading a variety of translations; for when one does so, he or she will gain new insights into the originally intended concepts of the inspired writings themselves. Though translations transcribe verses in varying ways or use differing vocabulary from one another, more often than not, the original idea of God's inspired Word remains. Comparing multiple translations often yields seeing a subject from variant angles, allowing for a broader understanding of any given text. There are many resources online that will enable one to look up Scriptures with dozens of translations side by side.

Now then, are some Bibles more accurate within their translations from the original languages than others? Sure, and this introduces the next process in finding the correct translation for us.

As we continue to learn and further our understanding of the original concepts and languages of the Bible, the correct translation for us may change. I hope there isn't a single translation that any given Christian solely relies on. While enacting this suggestion, I encourage others to investigate Scriptures more closely when they further their understanding within the text. When examining more specifically verses of interest, it would be helpful to look up the original Hebrew, Greek, or Aramaic to understand why any given translation transcribes verses as it does. For example, interlinear sources can also serve as a wonderful study tool in delineating the original texts' context. However, the point in this writer's opinion is that there is no such thing as a perfect translation; therefore, it is just a matter of our level of study as to how many resources we avail ourselves of.

Is there anything inherently wrong with favoring one particular translation over another? No, I usually encourage those who desire to further their understanding of prophecy to use a single translation. Often each Bible will use the same wording throughout when discussing nouns. This is a big help when researching connections between one text and another within the prophetic works. So in this way, a single translation can serve one well when studying prophecy concepts that interlink throughout the Scriptures. However, there is no such thing as a monopoly on God's Word; therefore, one should keep in mind that our favored translation is no more superior than perhaps another.

Our Father knew that variances would creep into the text over time and that His Word would not be a perfect iteration from the original inspired manuscripts. So detractors are correct when they say that today's translations are not identical to those transcribed initially; however, more often than not, they don't know what precisely they are arguing about. Simply translating any language from one to another requires using wording more suited to the language being translated into. That simple fact alone makes the newly translated work nonidentical to the original. If one were to translate word for word, the original context would be lost. And therein lies the intent of translating; it is the work of a translator to record the original language context, rather than a word for word copy. Anyone who is bilingual understands this concept quite readily.

Does this mean that today's modern translations are not faithful renditions of the original inspired writings? Absolutely not. You see, there are several significant factors that prove we have an accurate representation of God's initially inspired concepts, down through Bible translations we have today.

Firstly, in ancient Hebrew, it was customary for young men to write out the books of the Torah letter by letter when coming of age. If there was a single mistake or missing letter, the entire work was disposed of. Multiply that by the number of young men, and you can see a level of accuracy that accomplished a centuries-long lineage for the text over many generations.

Secondly, in translating ancient texts from one language to another, some of the foremost experts in their fields were used to accomplish this work. In so doing, it has been evident down through the ages that the level of care taken was that of the utmost importance by professional world-renowned transcribers.

Thirdly, we have greatly advanced our knowledge of this subject in our day, such as the discovery of texts from the Qumran valley that have given us centuries of previously unknown transcriptions, verifying the overall accuracy of documents handed down throughout the ages. This has done a great deal in silencing critics who had inferred that the texts we have currently could not have been accurate representations of the historically ancient originals. Upon finding these previously unknown Essene manuscripts, we were made aware that inaccuracies within our modern translations came down to something as simple as a name spelling or single word out of place. In no circumstance had a difference affected the original intent of the text itself. Far from the Bible being a work that has changed dramatically over time, it is a well-known fact that the ancient writings have remained grammatically intact throughout thousands of years of history.

There are influences of doctrine in every example of translation out there. If you hear someone put down a particular Bible for its doctrinal influences, well then, the same applies to their own preferred translation. This, unfortunately, is the result of human imperfection and prejudice of concepts. Ultimately though, even given our imperfections, this subject should not be about differences of doctrine but about commonalities between opposing views. What we should be doing is coming together as fellow Christians under a single faith, through our Lord Christ Jesus. "There is one body and one Spirit, just as you were called to one hope when you were called; one Lord, one faith, one baptism; one God and Father of all, who is over all and through all and in all" (Ephesians 4:4–6).

By faith in Christ Jesus we are saved, not through a corrected view of doctrine. Our Father knew well ahead of time there would be debates concerning His Word; this is an example of why salvation is not from having an accurate understanding of subjects in the Bible. As Christians, our salvation relies on faith in the sacrifice of our Lord Christ Jesus and His being raised on the third day, not on matters of contention that so often divide the Christian world. The comprehension of complexities within the writings is not what garners our Father's love. Let us heed our Lord's words by making disciples of others and not fostering a segregated attitude toward fellow Christians, but by finally gathering under one faith in our Lord Christ Jesus! (John 15:16).

Let us not get caught up in arguments about doctrine and controversies; let us find the commonalities that bind us all as Christians. Let us not have that *us versus them* mentality across divides, but instead, a welcome heart that identifies us as His disciples. "A new command I give you: Love one another. As I have loved you, so you must love one another. By this everyone will know that you are my disciples, if you love one another" (John 13:34–35). When speaking to others of faith, do not quarrel over differences of opinion, for this is against God's commands. Instead, focus on encouraging one another in love (1 Thessalonians 5:11).

> Keep reminding God's people of these things. Warn them before God against quarreling about words; it is of no value, and only ruins those who listen. (2 Timothy 2:14)

> But avoid foolish controversies and genealogies and arguments and quarrels about the law, because these are unprofitable and useless. Warn a divisive person once, and then warn them a second time. After that, have nothing to do with them. You may be sure that such people are warped and sinful; they are self-condemned. (Titus 3:9–10)

Don't have anything to do with foolish and stupid arguments, because you know they produce quarrels. And the Lord's servant must not be quarrelsome but must be kind to everyone, able to teach, not resentful. Opponents must be gently instructed, in the hope that God will grant them repentance leading them to a knowledge of the truth, and that they will come to their senses and escape from the trap of the devil, who has taken them captive to do his will. (2 Timothy 2:23–26)

All Scripture is God-breathed and is useful for teaching, rebuking, correcting and training in righteousness. (2 Timothy 3:16)

Chapter 3:7

# Who Is God?

There seems to be no more divisive subject in Christianity than the very word *God* itself. It is a good thing that our salvation relies on our faith in Christ Jesus rather than on any specific understanding of the term *God* used within Scripture. However, there is more variety of teachings on God than I believe any other subject in the Bible. So what do you say? Let us close the book on this subject here.

I would like to reiterate: While many very qualified teachers of the Word might suggest that one's salvation relies on a complete understanding of the substantive nature of God, it is of utmost importance to remember that our salvation is fixed on our faith in Christ Jesus having given His life on behalf of our sins and being raised on the third day, rather than on having any complete understanding of the relationship of Father to Son. "For it is by grace you have been saved, through faith—and this is not from yourselves, it is the gift of God" (Ephesians 2:8).

With that said, the debate within Scripture over titles given to God's headship has become a perpetual disputation, permeating the entire concept of who God really is. This, however, has clouded the very message of salvation itself and has unnecessarily introduced conflict and segregation within an otherwise singular faith. While some have made this a matter of complexity, the understanding of titles within the holy text need not be a subject of contention, for I find that in most cases, both sides would do well to combine their understandings of each other. All too often, those with conflicting opinions debate two sides of the same coin, describing the same God from a differing view. As I have said previously, Scripture is like a painting: we must step back to describe all brushstrokes as a singular work.

Since it is the nature of God that lies at the crux of this discussion, let us ask some qualifying questions to lay a foundation. Is the one God we should pray to made up of a Trinity, one God in three Persons? Is Jesus synonymous and part of the tetragrammaton of YHWH Himself? As well, did Christ Jesus have a heavenly preexistence before being born of Mary? These seem the prevailing debates surrounding the nature of God, and it will be these we shall address here.

Let us begin with that word *God* itself and the most appropriate text to start with, John 1:1: "In the beginning was the Word, and the Word was with God, and the Word was God." In this text, the "Word" is a translation from the Greek *Logos*, literally meaning a premise or logic. The Word here is the very intent of God Himself, the purpose of all things. This reasoning is highlighted in the third verse of John one. "Through him all things were made; without him nothing was made that has been made." It was by the Word all things were made, through Him and for Him. Therefore, the Word is the very envisage of God, in whom all Creation was intended.

It can be said definitively that the Logos, or Word here, describes Christ Jesus. In the fourteenth verse, we read, "The Word became flesh and made his dwelling among us" (John 1:14). As the very Word of God, Jesus became flesh to establish the pathway by which all mankind could receive salvation through faith, upon His Resurrection. Therefore, the Word who was in the beginning with God could be none other than Christ Jesus Himself.

While the concept of an Adoptionism view holds that Jesus was established as a conceptual Word at His birth, this idea denies a preexistence of the Word as a being and relies on the assumption that the Logos is merely an attribute, rather than a distinct consciousness. Clearly, Scripture supports a precognitive existence of the Word itself, before Christ Jesus even became flesh:

> "Very truly I tell you," Jesus answered, "before Abraham was born, I am!" (John 8:58)

> Then I was constantly at his side. I was filled with delight day after day, rejoicing always in his presence, rejoicing in his whole world and delighting in mankind. (Proverbs 8:30–31)

Rather than His Father indicating that He was merely prophesied to come, He existed before being born of Mary. "For he chose us in him before the creation of the world to be holy and blameless in his sight" (Ephesians 1:4).

> The next day John saw Jesus coming toward him and said, "Look, the Lamb of God, who takes away the sin of the world! This is the one I meant when I said, 'A man who comes after me has surpassed me because he was before me.'" (John 1:29–30)

And I heard a loud voice from the throne saying, "Look! God's dwelling place is now among the people, and he will dwell with them."
(Revelation 21:3)

God said to Moses, "I AM WHO I AM. This is what you are to say to the Israelites: 'I AM has sent me to you.'" (Exodus 3:14)

# Part Four
# *YHWH*

Chapter 4:1

# The Beginning

What is the beginning spoken of in John 1:1? Many theologians teach that this beginning was that of Genesis 1:1, "In the beginning God created the heavens and the earth." At face value, this seems a proper understanding; after all, the first verse of the Bible does speak of the beginning of the creation of the heavens and earth. However, when one understands that the Word is God's intention to create, then a belief that the Word always existed falls apart. If we believe creation in Genesis 1:1 was the beginning of Creation itself, and the Word was at the beginning of that Creation, then how could God's intent to create exist before the first creation if the very nature of the Word is God's intent to create?

This thought process presents a paradox for those understanding that the Word has always existed, as well as for those believing the Word had its beginning at the creation of the heavens and earth. For quite simply, Jesus indicates that the Word existed before the earth even was. "And now, Father, glorify me in your presence with the glory I had with you before the world began" (John 17:5). As the Word, Jesus says here that He existed before the heavens and earth were created. The heavens spoken of in the Creation account from Genesis refer to those physical features associated with the earth and visible from it. The Hebrew word used for heavens is *shamayim* and represents not the singular heavenly abode in which YHWH dwells, but simply a part of the Creation days of Genesis, the physical nature of this universe itself.

So if the Word existed before the intent to create the heavens and earth, that begs the question of what beginning John 1:1 is speaking of when it says, "In the beginning was the Word, and the Word was with God, and the Word was God" (John 1:1). If the Word is God's very intent to create, how could the Word exist before Creation? Conversely, how could the Word have always existed, eons before any intended creation?

The reason for this paradox is that the beginning spoken of in John 1:1 is not the same beginning spoken of in Genesis 1:1. This is why the book of John says, "the Word was with God," because He already existed previous to the creation of all things through Him. The only way the Word can be associated with a beginning is if God's intent to create existed before any creation through Him. Meaning, the Word had to exist before Creation in the Genesis account. YHWH never had a beginning; therefore, if the Word is not the beginning of the Creation account in Genesis, but existed beforehand, then the only solution is that the Word was the first intent of God to create before anything was created through Him.

As Sir Arthur Conan Doyle said, "Once you eliminate the impossible, whatever remains, no matter how improbable, must be the truth."

Chapter 4:2

# All Things Created Through Him

Someone at this point might say: "But doesn't John 1:3 indicate that Jesus never had a beginning? 'Through him all things were made; without him nothing was made that has been made'" (John 1:3). We must remember that not only were all letters capital in the original Greek, but the ancient texts were also written without punctuation. What we read in modern translations from the original Greek of John are, unfortunately, interpretations where a simple period or comma can change the entire meaning of the phrase or sentence. The only way to understand the sentence structure within the text's original intent is to understand the concepts which the writer is inferring. The ancient writers wrote in ideas without using the sentence structures we use today. Where we use punctuation to separate differing clauses, the ancient Greek writers wrote in streams of concepts. Case in point: When we read John 1:3, if we apply our own face-value understanding of, "Without him nothing was made, that was made," then we might believe the writer intends to suggest that nothing ever was created without Him; but is this the context in which this sentence is written?

First, at the start of this sentence, John indicates he is speaking of all things created through the Word, which defines that which is spoken of as coming into being. Then, given there was no punctuation in the original Greek, translations have ended that sentence as we now read it, believing the writer intended to suggest quite simply, "all things." The proper translation of John 1:3, however, should include the first two words of verse 4. In modern Bibles, normally the beginning of John 1:4 is the two Greek words, *en autō*, meaning through Him, in Him, or for Him. "In him was life, and that life was the light of all mankind" (John 1:4). However, when we properly end verse 3 with the first two words, *en autō* from verse 4, we have verse 3's original intent in its completion.

Given the context of Romans chapter 11, these three translations combined offer the best understanding of the original context of John 1:3. "For from him and through him and to him are all things" (Romans 11:36, ESV):

> Through Him, all things were created, and without Him, not even one thing came into being that was created through Him. (Joshua Stone)

> For the sake of Him all things were created, and without Him, not even one thing came into being that was created for Him. (Joshua Stone)

> On account of Him all things were created, and without Him, not even one thing came into being that was created on account of Him. (Joshua Stone)

This is the proper stream of context that John intended and is representative of Creation's conceptual precedence being spoken of as that which was created "through Him." Now does this indicate in any way that the Word never had a beginning?

Going back to verse 4 of John chapter 1: Once the first two words are removed and placed within their proper position at the end of John 1:3, the concept of verse 4 is now more precise and brings it more in line with the context of the first three verses:

> Life came about, and that life was the light of mankind. (Joshua Stone)

> Life was, and that life was the light of mankind. (Joshua Stone)

Now verse 5 completes the chain of context. "The light shines in the darkness, and the darkness has not overcome it" (John 1:5).

Many translations ignore and have removed an elementary word from the first two verses. In Greek, this word is *ton* and is representative of our English word *the*. However, this is a critical word that must remain within the translation to understand the relationship of the individuals spoken of. Here I have prepared more accurate translations of verses 1–5:

> In the beginning was the Word, and the Word was with the God, and the Word was God. He was in the beginning with the God. Through Him, all things were created, and without Him, not even one thing came into being that was created through Him. Life came about, and that life was the light of mankind. The light shines in the darkness, and the darkness has not overcome it. (Joshua Stone)

> In the beginning was the Word, and the Word was with the God, and the Word was God. He was in the beginning with the God. For the sake of Him, all things were created, and without Him, not even one thing came into being that was created for Him. Life was, and that life was the light of mankind. The light shines in the darkness, and the darkness has not overcome it. (Joshua Stone)

This distinction between Logos and *the* God is an essential one. The reason Jesus is never mentioned as the Almighty within the pages of the Bible becomes quite apparent as one considers countless incidences throughout Christ Jesus's life that quite frankly make it impossible for Him to be His Father. As an example: The Almighty cannot sin (Hebrews 6:18). If then Jesus was the Almighty, why would Satan tempt Him? If Jesus were incapable of sin, this would have been an absolute waste of time to have offered Him all the kingdoms of the world. Wouldn't Satan have known that the Almighty could not bow down and worship him? Clearly, Satan took advantage of his opportunities to sway a human individual capable of defying God, even though He never did.

Who did Jesus pray to? "At that time Jesus, full of joy through the Holy Spirit, said, 'I praise you, Father, Lord of heaven and earth, because you have hidden these things from the wise and learned, and revealed them to little children. Yes, Father, for this is what you were pleased to do'" (Luke 10:21).

Whose voice was heard from heaven declaring Jesus as His Son? "And a voice from heaven said, 'This is my Son, whom I love; with him I am well pleased'" (Matthew 3:17).

How could Jesus die if the Almighty cannot die? "Lord, are you not from everlasting? My God, my Holy One, you will never die" (Habakkuk 1:12).

Who raised Christ Jesus from the dead? "But God raised him from the dead, freeing him from the agony of death, because it was impossible for death to keep its hold on him" (Acts 2:24).

Why did He rebuke a man for calling him good by saying that only one is good, the Father? "Why do you call me good?" Jesus answered. "No one is good—except God alone" (Luke 18:19).

Why were there things Jesus did not know? "But about that day or hour no one knows, not even the angels in heaven, nor the Son, but only the Father" (Matthew 24:36).

Can the Father be tempted as Jesus was? "When tempted, no one should say, 'God is tempting me.' For God cannot be tempted by evil, nor does he tempt anyone" (James 1:13).

"Why were you searching for me?" he asked. "Didn't you know I had to be in my Father's house?" (Luke 2:49)

Chapter 4:3

# The Beginning of God's Creation

A chronological mind, therefore, would at this point consider further Christ's words in Revelation. "The words of the Amen, the faithful and true witness, the beginning of God's creation" (Revelation 3:14, ESV).

While again, some might suggest that Jesus here was speaking of the Creation account in Genesis, others may indicate He was speaking of His place of authority or right to rule. The Greek word here used as "beginning" is the word *archē*. While appearing a dozen times in the New Testament, there is only one place that uses this term to indicate someone's position of power; that is Luke 20:20, where its use was in conjunction with secular rulers within the Hebraic nation. In each of the remaining eleven verses, this Greek word denotes the start of something, such as is found here: "The beginning of the good news about Jesus the Messiah" (Mark 1:1).

However, we have a definitive understanding of the conceptual use of the Greek word *arche* used in the book of Revelation as beginning, from Colossians. "And he is the head of the body, the church; he is the beginning and the firstborn from among the dead, so that in everything he might have the supremacy" (Colossians 1:18). In seemingly identical context, Jesus is spoken of as the beginning in like manner, within both locations. As first in a sequence in the book of Colossians, and by exemplar in Revelation as well. It is clear: Christ Jesus is spoken of as the first of God's creation in life and rebirth, rather than any explanation of His position as ruler. Revelation does not mince words when discussing Christ Jesus's rulership. "They came to life and reigned with Christ a thousand years" (Revelation 20:4).

With this insight, it should become clear that the Word was the first intention of YHWH's creation. Before all things, He was. And by Him, and through Him, all things were created. That beginning the Word is associated with in John 1:1 can be only one beginning, the beginning of creation itself:

> The Lord brought me forth as the first of his works, before his deeds of old; I was formed long ages ago, at the very beginning, when the world came to be. When there were no watery depths, I was given birth, when

there were no springs overflowing with water; before the mountains were settled in place, before the hills, I was given birth, before he made the world or its fields or any of the dust of the earth. (Proverbs 8:22–26)

Chapter 4:4

# GOD, God, or god?

Is Jesus GOD in the first book of John, with all letters capitalized? Yes! You see, in the original Greek, all letters were capital, and therefore, capitalization is not an indicator of nature. The term *GOD* itself cannot indicate an individual's headship within any given text. Only the context allows for the conceptual understanding of the nature of the ones spoken of. Why, there are many gods according to Scripture; in fact, Satan is spoken of using the same Greek word *theos*, or god, as is the Word. "The god of this age has blinded the minds of unbelievers, so that they cannot see the light of the gospel that displays the glory of Christ, who is the image of God" (2 Corinthians 4:4).

We must separate from our minds the idea that our English word *God* is only used in association with the Almighty. When you understand that even Satan is spoken of using the same word *theos*, as is the Word in John 1:1, the word *God* alone cannot be used to indicate one's nature. We cannot determine ruling position in any given context without understanding the word's conceptual use in any given textual placement.

In our modern English, we capitalize the word *God* when discussing the Creator, showing our intent to indicate that this is the One who is over all things, the Giver of Life. Conversely, we write out Satan's status as god, without any capitalization, for he is the enemy of life, the original liar, who will be destroyed in due time. So when we apply our modern capitalization concepts to the original texts, personal interpretation creeps in. This is not a correct approach in understanding headship in the Bible, especially when two Gods are spoken of, as is the case in John 1:1. Instead, we want to precisely know what the text intends to teach us, not what our modern capitalization concepts should be.

There are yet others who transcribe the Word in John 1:1 as god, with no capitalization at all. Is this type of translation correct? Yes! We could translate the term as GOD, God, or god, and each would be equivalent. The term is only used here to indicate positions of power. When two or more are discussed within a text, only by understanding the context in which it is used can one understand the relationships and roles of the individuals spoken of. After all, is this not the very subject we are highlighting: Who is God? It behooves us to pay close attention here.

With this in mind, can we understand the moniker of God given to the Word as an indication that He never had a beginning? Is it merely for the fact that He is called God that we should understand He has always been? As an example, we read of Jesus as God in Hebrews, alongside God:

> In your relationships with one another, have the same mindset as Christ Jesus: Who, being in very nature God, did not consider equality with God something to be used to his own advantage; rather, he made himself nothing by taking the very nature of a servant, being made in human likeness. And being found in appearance as a man, he humbled himself by becoming obedient to death—even death on a cross! (Philippians 2:5–8)

Again, here we have Jesus spoken of as God, in singular identity, separate from the second, also called God. Therefore, to reiterate: The term *God* is not an indicator of divinity to anyone associated with it in Scripture. Conversely, does the concept of the Word having a beginning in any way detract from His divinity? Of course not. Our Lord Christ Jesus's divine nature is evident through His rightfully ordained rulership at baptism.

## Chapter 4:5

# The Trinity

Many argue that Jesus is the same individual or a personage of the tetragrammaton YHWH in the Old Testament. Foremost within their argument is simply the fact that He is spoken of with that same ruling term of *God*; however, it must be understood that one cannot combine two individually spoken of entities into a singular being, based on the fact they are both spoken of as ruling. The term *theos* is not an identifier of the Almighty alone and cannot be used to represent headship among all entities.

Is Jesus to be worshiped in place of the Father? Should our prayers be directed to Him? Jesus Himself never indicated mankind should worship Him in prayer; instead, He quite clearly stated otherwise when He gave direction on how to pray. "This, then, is how you should pray: 'Our Father in heaven, hallowed be your name'" (Matthew 6:9).

The tetragram YHWH or JHVH represents the Father's name in Hebrew. In English, the most common translations are Yahweh, or the more widely used form, Jehovah. Simply Father is appropriate as well, for even Jesus Himself indicated that no one should call Him Father. "And do not call anyone on earth 'father,' for you have one Father, and he is in heaven" (Matthew 23:9).

Some argue that we do not have an accurate understanding of how God's name was pronounced among the ancient Hebrews and suggest we shouldn't even use it at all. In reality, it is not the pronunciation that is important, but the intent of the prayerful. Even my own personal name is pronounced differently among many of my friends from around the world. It is the intent behind its use that is important, not the pronunciations from the individual languages it was spoken from. After all, it was God Himself who confused the languages of Babel. He knows His name will be pronounced differently among differing tongues. It is not the pronunciation that is important; it is the understanding behind it.

While it is through the Lord Christ Jesus our prayers are directed to the Father, it is Jehovah we should be addressing in prayer. "So with you: Now is your time of grief, but I will see you again and you will rejoice, and no one will take away your joy. In that day you will no longer ask me anything. Very truly I tell you, my Father will give you whatever you ask in my name" (John 16:22-23). Being the pathway unto the Father, we offer our prayers directed to the Father Himself in the name of Jesus.

With that said, the Lord's disciples spoke directly to Jesus after His resurrection on many occasions. Stephen, even before his martyrdom, called out to the Lord to receive his spirit. "While they were stoning him, Stephen prayed, 'Lord Jesus, receive my spirit'" (Acts 7:59). So it seems clear that while informally our words to the Lord Christ Jesus are appropriate, it is our worship in prayer that we should direct to our Father.

What are we told the Father is in relation to the Son? We are told God is the God of God. This is explained quite well throughout Scripture. "You love righteousness and hate wickedness; therefore God, your God, has set you above your companions by anointing you with the oil of joy" (Psalm 45:7; see also Hebrews 1:9). Christ Jesus has a God! Though Jesus rules, He has a ruler. This text in Psalms clearly indicates a rank higher for the God of the first God, as the context shows the superiority of one God over the other, when the first God is spoken of as worshiping His God, Jehovah. As well, we know He prayed using His Father's name because Jesus used the name of His God when teaching. "I made known to them your name, and I will continue to make it known, that the love with which you have loved me may be in them, and I in them" (John 17:26, ESV).

There is nothing within the text to indicate that Jesus was ever worshiped before He came to the earth. "And again, when God brings His firstborn into the world, he says, 'Let all God's angels worship him'" (Hebrews 1:6). You see, it is at the point of His earthly life that Jesus is said to have been given reverence once He is set above His companions at His anointing baptism.

For there is one God and one mediator between
God and mankind, the man Christ Jesus.
(1Timothy 2:5)

Chapter 4:6

# Trinitarian vs. Unitarian

Throughout my many years of study, I have spoken with Trinitarian and Unitarian alike and have studied in depth the very details of each understanding as well. While each has the saving grace of faith in Christ, each could learn a great deal from the other if more would simply listen with hearts open instead of attempting to prove one's own insights. Finding commonality often leads to more productive engagements than does contention (1 Peter 3:8–17).

I often hear from those who believe in one of the many forms of the Trinity who quote Scriptures that they feel support their identification of Jesus as the Almighty. In each instance, it is merely a matter of the commenter interpreting a single brushstroke rather than considering the entire painting. "Now the Berean Jews were of more noble character than those in Thessalonica, for they received the message with great eagerness and examined the scriptures every day to see if what Paul said was true" (Acts 17:11).

Case in point: Often this Scripture is quoted: "I and the Father are one" (John 10:30). Yet was our Lord indicating that He and His Father were the same entity? He clarifies this statement just a few chapters later. "My prayer is not for them alone. I pray also for those who will believe in me through their message, that all of them may be one, Father, just as you are in me and I am in you" (John 17:20). Jesus prays that His disciples be one, just as He and His Father are one. The disciples could not be of one singular entity. No, Christ Jesus and His Father are one in agreement, in solidarity. The Bible is not a collection of verses; it is a combined cohesive whole.

Another example might be, "But about the Son he says, 'Your throne, O God, will last for ever and ever; a scepter of justice will be the scepter of your kingdom'" (Hebrews 1:8). As God, the Word sits on the throne of God; therefore, He must be one and the same, right? No, in fact, we read that He is actually sitting upon His God's throne, His Father's. "To the one who is victorious, I will give the right to sit with me on my throne, just as I was victorious and sat down with my Father on his throne" (Revelation 3:21). The throne of God also becomes the Word's throne when He is crowned as king over a given kingdom. The throne, as a symbol, is that of the seat of rulership over Creation.

Chapter 4:7

# Christ Jesus Rules

When the Word is given rulership over all things, all are subject to Him, except the one who subjected all things unto Him. "Now when it says that 'everything' has been put under him, it is clear that this does not include God himself, who put everything under Christ. When He has done this, then the Son himself will be made subject to him who put everything under him, so that God may be all in all" (1 Corinthians 15:27–28). All things are put under Christ, except Christ's God Jehovah, at which point at the end of the age, once all things are given back over to the Father once again, Jehovah Himself will be all things in all!

Again, does this understanding in any way lessen Christ Jesus's deification? No, for Jesus is reverenced as God by all He currently rules over. And one day He will rule all Creation in heaven and earth in like manner, when all things are put in subjection to Him, except the one who subjected all things unto Him, God Almighty.

In the matter of Thomas calling Jesus his God, he could rightly do so, for He is, and always has been God from the beginning of Creation itself (John 20:28). Jesus is not, however, by any means, part of any numerous definitions of a Trinity, a concept established among early peoples of Mesopotamia and then adopted down through the ages by many institutional arrangements. Neither the word *Trinity* nor the concept are found anywhere within the pages of the holy writings.

In recognition of a previously unrealized conceptual understanding of the rule of our Lord Himself, I will endeavor to appoint a new neologism here, known as Coronationist. This seems fitting, for in a Coronationism understanding, the very first creation by God, known as the Word and God, is given rulership over His God's kingdom when anointed and reverenced directly by its subjects, as God. Then, one day still yet future, He will be given kingship over the earthly realm at the arrival of His Final Kingdom!

> I am coming soon. Hold on to what you have, so that no one will take your crown. (Revelation 3:11)

In the last days, God says, I will pour out my Spirit on all people. (Acts 2:17)

# Index

7 Times .................85
7 Years .................89
40 Days .................85
42 Months .............70
70 Weeks ...............93
666 ......................137
777 Days ...............96
1260 Days .............69
1290 Days .............63
1335 Days .............65
2300 Days .............66
2520 Days .............85
144,000 ...............112
Adoptionism .......191
Almighty .............205
Altar ...................111
Apostasy .............135
Appointed Times...76
Ark .......................66
Asara B'Tevet .......86
Asceticism ............10

Atonement ..........77
Babylon ................84
Beasts ...................79
Beginning ...........197
Capstone .............164
Chronology ..........63
Conscience ..........13
Contentment ..........2
Cornelius ..............96
Covenant ..............95
Creation ..............197
Dedication ...........13
Divinity ..............215
Earth ....................55
Eden .....................19
Eighth King .........80
Elijah ..................153
End Timeline ........98
Enmity .................38
Entertainment ......16
Essenes ...............183

| | |
|---|---|
| Eternal Life .......... 53 | Justification ......... 43 |
| Fasts ..................... 76 | Knowledge ............ 22 |
| Feasts ................... 76 | Laver ................... 111 |
| Firstfruits ............. 76 | Life ....................... 46 |
| Forgiveness ............ 1 | Logos ................... 191 |
| Forsaken ............. 174 | Love ........................ 6 |
| Gethsemane ....... 173 | Lunisolar .............. 77 |
| God ..................... 213 | Maccabean Revolt 65 |
| Greed ................... 36 | Martin Luther ....... 46 |
| Hades ................. 122 | MOL .................... 140 |
| Hanukkah ............ 78 | Most Holy Place .113 |
| Holidays ............... 75 | Nebuchadnezzar ...83 |
| Holy Days ............ 75 | New Creation ....... 54 |
| Holy of Holies ... 113 | North ................... 80 |
| Holy Place ............ 66 | Paradise ................ 57 |
| Holy Spirit ........... 15 | Passover ............... 76 |
| Horn ..................... 79 | Peace ...................... 1 |
| Image of God ....... 35 | Pentecost .............. 77 |
| Images ................. 37 | Prayer ................. 217 |
| Indulgences .......... 10 | Preface ................ 100 |
| Inequality ............. 30 | Prophecy .............. 64 |
| Interlinear .......... 181 | Pushing ................ 80 |
| Internet ................ 30 | Qumran .............. 183 |
| Introduction .......... 7 | Redeemed ............. 43 |
| Israel .................. 127 | Reformation ......... 43 |
| Jews .................... 129 | Resurrection ....... 117 |
| JHVH ................. 218 | Rosh Hashanah ...101 |
| John 1:1 ............. 191 | Rule ...................... 27 |
| Joshua Stone ...... 169 | Rulership ............ 227 |

Sacrifice ................67
Sadness ..................27
Sanctuary ............109
Satan .....................20
Saved ....................45
Sin .........................9
Smyrna ..................86
South ....................80
Suffering ................1
Sukkot ..................79
Tabernacle ............77
Temple ..................71
Thief ....................103
Times ....................69

Transfiguration ..156
Transfigured .........86
Translations ........179
Tree of Knowledge 19
Trinity ................217
Trumpets ..............77
Two Witnesses ...147
Unitarianism ......223
Unleavened Bread 76
War .......................80
Word ...................191
Works ...................43
YHWH ...............218
Yom Kippur ..........78

Peace be with you through Christ Jesus.

Joshua Stone

www.ingramcontent.com/pod-product-compliance
Lightning Source LLC
Chambersburg PA
CBHW071811080526
44589CB00012B/754